# THE ULTIMATE JOURNEY

AN EARTH TRAVELLERS GUIDE TO
AWAKENING

Frank Di Genova

Allow Right Now Publishing
Toronto, Canada

Frank Di Genova/Allow Right Now Publications
Toronto, Canada
www.frankdigenova.com

Book Layout ©2016 BookDesignTemplates.com

Book Cover Design ©2016 Rosario Carrabino

Publisher Logo ©2016 i catching designs

The Ultimate Journey/ Frank Di Genova. — 1st ed.
ISBN 978-0-9951596-1-7

Allow Right Now
**PUBLISHING**

*To Doug*
*oh boy*
*today we write da*
*book. To a great*
*guy. warmest*
*Frank D'Genova*

This book is dedicated to all of you who desire to find the answers to life's mysteries and questions.

To every seeker that yearns to self-realize, and has the courage to face their fear, and delve into the layers of their ignorance and self-doubt.

For those who persevere, even when all hope seems gone, and to those who trust and follow their heart.

This book is also dedictaed to my mother, my son and to the Higher Self dwelling in of each of you.

Namaste

# Contents

# FOREWORD

You will be 'soul-touched' by Frank's journey, so much so, that it will continue to resonate with you long after the last page has been turned. As Carl Jung said, "Your vision will become clear only when you can look into your own heart. Who looks outside, dreams, who looks inside, awakens."

When Frank asked me if I would consider writing the foreword for this book, I immediately responded with an honoured and humbled *yes*! After nearly a decade from first meeting Frank, it is clear that Divine intervention took over and moved the 'peaces' into play so that they could become what they are today—an Earth traveller's guide to awakening. Frank speaks with candour about the journey that he was birthed into and has travelled.

A natural raconteur, Frank openly shares his empath experiences and karmic lessons that necessitated his soul growth from learning to portage through the rapid headwaters called the Earth realm. His path has seen him transition from being immersed and barely surviving an existential life of intolerance, negligence, ignorance and carelessness through to awakening and emerging, to living and thriving with patience, discipline, maturity, and responsibility.

In a way, this is a Love story—a raw and authentic Love story that will give you a renewed sense of remembering why you're here in this Earth realm and your purpose for returning to Love. You will know that you too can transcend any fears, self-loathing, self-abuse, self-neglect, and self-rejection that may have been defining your life and your very way of existing. Frank shares on an intimate level how he healed, released and transformed into his awakened state. He continues to heal his life, through forgiveness, compassion, and love of himself first. In doing so, he is experiencing profound understanding at a much deeper level in his life's journey, as well as others.

Make no mistake, his mission and journey, in an epic way reflect what all of us need to know as we travel the path of awakening and of becoming our service to others. As a culture, we have become conditioned to be selfish, and to be of service to ourselves to such an extent that our fellow Being's presence and desires have become nothing more than obstacles to be managed and navigated. It takes great courage to awaken fully, and great patience to allow the process to be what it is. The old conditioning (beliefs and behaviour) takes time to unravel and strip away, but time is what we have in this reality; time is this present moment. The inner trip that Frank has taken brings you to knowing who you truly are, and that is the most important truth that one can attain on this awakening journey.

Frank shares his travels of the inner path, escorting the reader through the irrefutable knowing that we are all pure Love. This path ultimately leads to the discovery of non-attachment

and profound understanding that the source of love, peaceful-
ness, acceptance, wisdom, compassion and awareness resides
within each and every one of us.

'In-joy' Frank's consciousness blossoming book. Don't be
surprised if you find yourself cheering him and his spiritual
essence onwards, while recognizing how Divine intervention
takes over and places us exactly where we need to be to experience the ultimate awakening and soul growth. Frank details the
path of reassessing the human terrain—what we believed in and
what we trusted, and how clarity and truth add deeper meaning
to our lives. Evidenced throughout his words are life circumstances and happenings all manifesting with the intention of
goading and guiding us to find the answers within.

The world has been waiting for this kind of work—an in-
sightful guidebook to bring the reader through awareness,
awakening, heart consciousness and spiritual authenticity. The
degree of devotion, dedication and heart wisdom are gently revealed as Frank journeys the Earth realm, to reveal the evidence
of soul brilliance that is constantly empowering and encouraging every heartbeat along the way.

This is an Earth traveller's guidebook and travelogue to rec-
ognize the path of darkness and unawareness to reveal the ray
of light (hue-man), awakened (free) and creative Being that is
your birthright. Find your truth by realizing who you are at the
deepest level—Love! You too can live the life that you truly came
to Earth to live.

Theresa Marcotte
Author, Speaker, Spiritual Guide-Teacher & Energy Intuitive
Whitby, ON
www.SwanSource.ca

# ACKNOWLEDGMENTS

To all those that made this book possible:

*Luke Di Genova* for trusting and having faith in me. From the moment you were born, you have positively changed my life in ways that I could never have imagined.

*Theresa Marcotte* for your gracious foreword, patience, and profound insights which have helped me distil the wisdom I sought which was inside me all along. Deepest respect.

*Leanda Michelle* for helping me navigate through the arduous process of writing this book. Special thanks for being my editor and sounding board. You're sensitivity and understanding of this material were invaluable assets in refining this manuscript.

*Judith Robuliak* for being my beta reader, and special consultant. Your extraordinary insights and sense of energy and flow, was imperative for me to reflect my truest intentions.

To: *Jim Bean, Rein Kuris, Andrew Levitt,* and *Donna Tammela,* for your years of friendship, teaching and profundity.

To: Heather Hannan and Catherine Varga from The Sound Reiki Institute, for your friendship and teaching.

To my friends, family, spiritual teachers and Sedona Tribe, for co-creating and sharing life's journey with me.

Finally, I would like to express my love and gratitude to my *mother* and *father* for bringing me into this world, without you this book wouldn't be possible, and to the greatest mentor of all—Life itself.

# INTRODUCTION

I had a dream one night. I woke at 3 am. My body was too tired to move. It didn't matter. Something forced me out of bed and to my computer. The words I typed into the browser still elude me. The tale they led me to was a message I will never forget.

Once there was a poor man in India. One night he left his house to steal some fruit from the king's garden to feed his family. He climbed the palace wall and then quickly scaled a fruit tree as he heard a guard fast approaching. There he stayed until morning. Early the next day the king was walking by with his advisor who was giving him spiritual advice. The man hiding in the tree couldn't believe the lies the king was being told. "This is not right," he thought. With no concern of getting caught he climbed down the tree.

"Your majesty I am very sorry to have trespassed on your land, please forgive me. I am poor and only wanted some fruit to give to my hungry family. Do to me as you wish, but I couldn't keep hiding knowing your advisor was telling you lies."

The king questioned his advisor, and banished him. In gratitude he made the poor man his primary confidante. His family was welcomed and granted a place of honour in his palace.

This story touched me deeply. I was hiding in fear, afraid to stand in my truth, anxious of being exposed and judged. I have tasted the forbidden fruit. I am no longer ashamed. This is my journey.

What is the Ultimate Journey? I believe it's different for all of us. Each traveller has their own path and lessons to learn. The journey is not a destination, but a process of letting go of our false beliefs, limitations and unworthiness. Our mission is to release the baggage we have accumulated throughout our lives, unlearning the corrupted programming instilled by the ones before us, and before them. What if we have the ability to change it all? To write a new story, one that empowers us instead of keeping us trapped inside its mental prison?

It has taken all of my life to understand what to write in this book. In it I share with you what I've learned so far. This narrative is about my process, and in no way am I about telling you what to do. At times it will appear as such. However, my intent is to convey my theories with as little fluff as possible. Most times, the only way to fully grasp a lesson is by experience. Ultimately, it's through compassion and by loving yourself. No matter how many books I've read, or heard from people that knew better, I never listened. It seemed I chose to learn my lessons the hard way. What did others know, this was my life. This book is my humble attempt to share what I've learned without preaching. It comes from my heart, and from my desire to connect with yours. You are my brothers and sisters, equals, nomads walking together on this journey.

This book is unique, as is the author, and is written as such. It starts with a brief account of my life, addressing only the major highlights. Eleven more chapters and possibly a sequel would be needed to cover it in more detail. In addition, the information I share had to be condensed, as a whole book could be written on each subject. My intent was to distil small fragments of my life and lace them with theory, to help you relate. I don't know all the answers, and can only tell you what has worked for me. What I do know is I am no longer a victim needing sympathy and approval. Fear doesn't control me. These words will one day be declared with absolute candour—for now they represent my best efforts.

This tale is not about me, it's about us as a whole and the similarities of our struggle. When we share our experiences, we help each other. I know many of you have had a harder go than I have, and in no way is this account any attempt to trump yours. My design is transparency, authenticity, compassion and understanding. My desire with this book is that it resonates with you.

The next eleven chapters address the many facets of the human journey. They consist of the following:

The second chapter implies we are more than our body. It explains the process of how our early needs, if not met, can subsequently affect our lives. I shed light on how our true nature has been forgotten, how we no longer believe we are spirit having a human experience.

Chapter three explores the possibility that we may be under a mass hypnosis, for the purpose of keeping us distracted, conditioned and unknowingly trapped.

The fourth chapter takes a look at our darker aspects, and how they keep us bound by fear, fuelling our sense of separateness.

Chapter five reveals how we fall into patterns, habits and addictions. I write about the different ways we use to distract ourselves from facing painful memories.

Chapter six describes relationships and how they are essential in knowing who we are. I reflect on their meaning and purpose, both from past and future perspectives. We are evolving and so are relationships—our roles have changed and continue to do so.

Chapter seven explains the theory of energy and vibration, how it works, and how it affects us. I raise the possibility that we may be living in a holographic reality, and what we feel is real may not necessarily be. I speak about good and evil, religion and spirituality—again from different perspectives.

Life is a river, it's about being in flow with it... or not. Chapter eight meanders through this concept, introducing the first of many meditations and exercises mentioned in this book.

Chapter nine explains why it's hard to change our behaviour. You'll read about focus and persistence. It introduces a fun and powerful technique to break out of limiting patterns.

Chapters nine to eleven reshape the paradigm into a how-to handbook. These chapters contain meditations, exercises, and ways of raising our vibration so we can ascend from our past conditioning.

Chapter's ten and eleven present ways in which we can raise our energy and dissolve what has become dense. This stagnant energy is what keeps us stuck. These chapters are a mini-workbook, containing exercises that can change how we live, think and eat.

Chapter twelve invites the imagination to envision what it may be like to live in a new energy, embracing a journey of self-exploration.

I am extremely grateful for being given the opportunity to look back on my life through a different lens. Had I chose to stay the victim, then writing this book wouldn't be possible. The expectation that life owed me something would have interfered with its process. Reading hundreds of books, attending countless workshops, and having a persistent thirst for knowledge has brought me here.

Being a hairstylist for thirty years has offered me great insight into the human condition. There is magic that happens when a client sits in my chair—it's more than a haircut. Something happens when you touch a person, especially their hair. They open up to you, bare their soul and trust you. This is not always the case as some, when vulnerability draws close, shut off even more. There is a common narrative woven within the tapestry of the human experience, and it becomes evident when you are afforded over forty-five thousand interviews. It doesn't matter what walk of life one is from, we all share similar feelings and emotions.

We all have a story, each unique, yet the same in many ways. Tears, laughter and the search for love permeate them all.

Every one of us holds a distinct and intimate account of our life's journey that has shaped us into who we are today. This is my story, and I hope it resonates with you. May it rouse dormant aspects within, wanting to awaken and express themselves. I offer you my narrative... this is my write of passage.

# CHAPTER ONE

# MY STORY

*"You can never feel, the pain I have inside, searching for the answers, I don't want to run and hide anymore." Excerpt from the song 'Shine' by Frank Di Genova 1984*

Ever since I was a child, the feeling of being different from everyone else was apparent to me. It wasn't until later when I realized I was more empathic than the norm. Not only did I acknowledge what others were feeling, but I felt it too. I wanted to fix them and ease their pain. Accepting this wasn't easy, it took me a long time to stop punishing myself for it. My parents wouldn't have understood. They were normal, I wasn't. They must have wondered what they got themselves into having me. Their beloved son getting drunk at two years old, stealing a car at three, and going for joyride at five. Six years had passed, and no jail time—success.

Capturing the attention of cute girls was easy. I'd smile at them, and if they smiled back (they usually did) I'd look up their skirts. The next step was crucial. I'd look them in the eyes, tilt their face gently to one side, close my eyes, and kiss them gently on the lips. King Kong would have pounded his chest in celebration. I'd just rubbed mine and let out a satisfied "ahhh." Five year olds don't typically behave like that do they?

On one occasion, my parents were visiting relatives—everyone was in the kitchen. Being a curious monkey, I set off to explore their house on my own. It wasn't long before I found and ate too many liquor filled chocolates. The sweetness must have disguised the burn. It was my first taste of alcohol, and definitely not my last.

I have no memory of my first trip to Italy, or of my grand theft auto. My parents and I were in Rome. We were waiting in the lobby at Fiumicino, Leonardo da Vinci International Airport for our flight home. If they had child leashes available back then, my parents wouldn't have hesitated to harness me. I ran ahead. They caught up with me in the gift store, and pulled me away—our plane was boarding. As we entered the gate I felt it was a great time to make an announcement. "Papa, ho comparato una macchina." In English... "Daddy, I bought a car." It was made of high quality metal, the model car was a red Ferrari. My father looked horrified and my mother, embarrassed. There was no way to return it, the plane was leaving. Isn't that how you bought things? What was money, anyway? How they didn't notice it was in my hands remains a mystery to me. To this day, money has never been my main goal in life, nor has stealing for that matter—with the exception of a few occasions.

A couple of years later my uncle was picking his son up from my grandmother's house, and left me alone in his car. I don't know if the ignition was on, or if the shifter in a 1964 Chevy Impala SS convertible could be disengaged manually. Never leave a monkey alone in a car, especially one like me, because I found a way. The car was parked on a sloped driveway with just enough gravity to get it rolling back onto the street, and to the other side of the road. The neighbours tree absorbed the impact of the crash despite the fact that the car was heading straight for the house. My uncle watched in horror from the top of the driveway.

I was a charismatic little boy, and won the hearts of everyone I met. In short, I was a spoilt brat. Little Frankey, naive and mischievous, always stirred the pot—a total badass. One time, in my father's salon, five year old me walked in with my mother on a visit. Perm fumes led me straight to the back room where I told my father, "Kick this lady out, she stinks!" I told it like it was. I still do, yet it's with charm and without malice.

That all changed at age eleven when my wonderful sister was born, altering my world forever. The attention was on her, and no longer on me. I reverted back to being a child, perhaps to reclaim the attention I'd lost. Instead of the happy-go-lucky little boy, I became a sensitive puddle of emotions, afraid to leave my playpen. Armour was slowly crafted, and little Frankey learned how to wear it. Time passed, and life went on. Things were good on the outside. However, no one knew what was going on inside. My sister and I were very close growing up, and not once did envy or jealously get in the way of that. There was no blame, just hurt. It was my show—what happened?

Going to school without knowing a word of English, wasn't easy for me. I knew a few words: hello, goodbye, and a few phrases from my favourite cartoon. Communicating was difficult and is probably why at times I used to stutter and suffer from anxiety when I spoke. Crying is universal, and understood in all languages, and exactly what I did when the school bus driver didn't stop at my drop off. He must not have understood, "qui, qui, fermati qui!" ("here, here, stop here!") The guy drove around town three times, with a crying five year old chirping like a bird in mating season. This is one of the many times my voice wasn't heard. The horror my mom must have felt when her son didn't come home. I returned the favour by kidnapping a little girl in my grade one class, bringing her home to play with me. Her mom had been waiting for her at school not knowing where she was... every parent's nightmare. My mother tried driving my new girlfriend home, only she didn't know where home was. The situation was sorted out eventually.

Crying and seduction were tools I'd learned early in life, and were passionate ways for me to connect with others. Why wasn't everyone emotionally sensitive like me? Why didn't they care for others like I did? How could people be so cold and selfish? Couldn't they feel compassion for another?

I trusted adults, believing they had it all figured out, that they knew everything. I quickly learned adults didn't have it all together, they were just as messed up as the rest of us. After many disappointing experiences of being let down, I started closing off, and that shinning light slowly faded.

I was often teased in grade school, got beat up for having long hair and was asked if I was a girl. Frankey is also a female name. Walking home from school without an incident was considered a victory. There would be days when my anxiety was so high I'd skip school and hide in my parent's garage, or the medical building where I got my weekly allergy injections. One day I got caught. My excuse, I blacked out and laid in a snow bank all day. That freaked my parents out alright. I often complained of dizziness and feeling like I was two seconds behind everything, which was true. After many tests, and an electroencephalogram (EEG), it was concluded there was nothing wrong with me. That was their opinion.

My parents, teachers and friends, including me, spelled my name, Frankie. It wasn't until I found my birth certificate that the true spelling was revealed... Frankey... what? I was devastated. Everyone had lied to me, even my parents. My father had made the decision to be different, creative, and had spelled my name like monkey. Was it fate that Chinese astrology, my supraorbital ridge, and what I called myself as a child resembled a primate? I sure acted like one. Frankey and monkey both contain the word key. Finding the *key* to unlock my ignorance was something I endeavoured to do.

I have forgotten most of my teen years. Perhaps this was my way of coping. I didn't want to remember. What I do recall was drinking, a lot. It was my way to escape, so was listening to heavy metal music. Pretending the pain wasn't there was next to impossible. Numbing it was my best option. I didn't want to feel anything anymore. Thank God needles freaked me out, or playing darts would have been my next choice after booze. Drinking worked best to anesthetize me. The trouble was the pain was always one step ahead. What was so bad in my life that I felt this way, why was I so angry? There were things to be proud of. I excelled in sports, especially hockey and was always the fastest skater. At age thirty-four I was clocked at just over fourteen seconds around the rink. In 2002 Sami Kapanen was crowned NHL's fastest skater at 14.039 seconds. I wonder how fast I'd have been at sixteen.

High school wasn't kind, and I found it no easier fitting in. That didn't stop me from trying. It was all about status and how good you looked. For some it's still the case, although not so much for me now. If my hair didn't turn out right, I'd skip that day. It was a new excuse, yet another emerging pattern. Do you remember Jordache or Sergio Valente jeans? You do, don't you? Admit it, you probably laid flat on your bed, with your breath sucked in, and a metal coat hanger looped into your zipper so you could pull them up. Mine were tight but not that tight—not good for the balls. Speaking of balls, there are pictures floating around to prove I had them. Imagine an Adidas three quarter t-shirt exposing my lower abdomen, short shorts that were to my crotch and white striped sweat socks pulled up as high as they could go. My hair was long and cut into a mullet, exposing my left pierced stud earring. To top it off, I wore white running shoes and mirrored sunglasses. Out of the many styles I fashioned, this took the cake for the most whacked. Looking at those pictures embarrasses me, not the me now, but the poor tortured soul that tried a little too hard.

I was the class clown and the party animal. Humour was my shield and helped me to fit in. My childhood idol was Ozzy Osbourne. Only later did I find out why. He too, suffered from low self-esteem, was beat up in school, stuttered and used humour to gain approval from his peers. I didn't have dyslexia or attention deficit disorder like he did, but I sure drank like him. Some people say I sing like Ozzy. I agree, but try not to. Even to this day, I make a conscious effort not to sound like him... I'm finding my own voice. Writing music, lyrics, and poems was my passion, and allowed me to express my cries for help and desire to hide. They were my attempts to be heard—a peek into my authentic self and opportunity to gain approval. But God forbid if anyone should see or hear me, I was too fragile for criticism. It never stopped me praying for the right person to notice and accept me for who I was, because I couldn't.

The years before my sister was born allowed me lots of time to be alone with myself. I didn't have an idle mind—my imagination conjured up fantasy worlds. I'd slay dragons, and was the hero who saved the day. It was a great way to escape this world—one I felt wasn't mine. Everything was a canvas to me, a blank space in which to draw and make toys from—there were no limitations. Every one of my toys was dismantled and put back together. I had to know how they worked, how life itself worked. Sometimes I couldn't put them back together. They were broken, like Humpty Dumpty... like little Frankey.

I was the cool guy, always happy and smiling—the only thing missing was my Oscar statuette for best actor in the movie, Faking My Life. Little did anyone know, I would later go home and have a breakdown. A total meltdown. A self-hating anger fuelled interrogation, where I blamed myself and God. I yelled at the top of my lungs. *"Why was I even born? Why did you even make me? Why couldn't you have taken me instead of my brother?"* I called on a God that couldn't be seen or heard, and unleashed every foul and disgusting word one could imagine. I was convinced I was being tortured for His sick amusement, punished for some crime I knew nothing about. *"Why is everyone pretending to be okay, when I can feel they're not. Why don't I fit in? Why don't I count?* My anger and self-hatred manifested all over my face—on my forehead, temples and down my cheeks as hundreds of boiling pimples. I hated me.

I've always wanted to become a rock star. I partied like one, so why not go all the way. Imagine all the money, the parties and the women. My bedroom walls were full of playboy centrefolds, and were the kinds of women I could have. Reality, of course, stung so psychology became my second choice—I wanted to know how people ticked. Since school wasn't my thing, and nothing else interested me—I didn't know what I wanted to become—I took the easy way out. My father's pockets were lined with wads of cash. Women were throwing themselves at him. He owned a hair salon and I wanted in on that. Long hair, female name and a career associated with being gay further pigeonholed me into a stereotype.

As much as I disliked being a stylist, I learned a lot about people, they opened up to me and trusted me. I got to see what was really hidden beneath their exterior. I loved giving advice, and found my empathic ability was finally being put to good use. Perhaps I did become a psychologist after all. I noticed most people weren't happy, although they pretended to be.

How could they accept being unhappy? Did they believe it was their fate? Why didn't they do anything about it? Maybe they were up for an Oscar as well? Faking my happiness though, was taking a toll. I was dying inside. Deep down I craved something much more profound, and hungered for something that couldn't be seen.

Pain often followed me, taking refuge on my lower back. However on one particular day the pain seized my neck. It was so stiff that doing hair was quite the chore. I moved like a robot. It wasn't fun. Next door to the salon was a café. Our back doors shared a common hallway, where we would often visit behind the scenes. When one of the staff noticed my stiffness, she offered to massage my neck. She said, "I'm good at massage and practise on my cats, they love it." Her attempt didn't help, although I thanked her for it. That *pain in the neck*, though, changed my life forever. In the seating area was a woman having lunch. She noticed I was getting a massage in the back hallway and offered to help.

"I'm a Reiki Master, and can help you," her words were soft, gentle and filled with compassion. "What's Reiki?" I countered. She told me to sit down, relax, close my eyes, and breathe. She laid her hands on my neck and upper back. Intense heat permeated my upper body. I began feeling nauseous, weak, and broke into a cold sweat. The nape of my neck tingled. There was love in those hands—unconditional love—and I surrendered to them. The moment I fully trusted and let go, the pain was gone. If I didn't experience it for myself, I wouldn't have believed it. "How can I pay you?" was my first thought. She looked into my eyes and said, "This is my gift to you."

Visiting the spiritual bookstore in-between clients became a daily ritual for me, and was a three minute walk from the salon. There I found answers, which led to more questions. My thirst grew. The staff got to know me very well. I became a spiritual-junkie, an insatiable sponge. My hands must have picked up each and every book they had, numbering in the thousands, until the store closed down. I read about everything and anything. These books added new meaning to my life and I felt destined to become enlightened. This was my way out of suffering, so was wanting to get married and have a family.

I got married at twenty-four, bought a house at twenty-five and welcomed my son in to the world when I was twenty-seven. It seemed like all my prayers had been answered. Everything I'd ever wanted came true, and in record time. Was I grateful? Yes and no... the void was still there, gnawing at me from the inside. There had to be more. Was this all there was to life? Was this *happiness*? I loved my wife and my in-laws. In fact my parents loved them all too. So what was my problem? This was the script I'd been taught. It was what I was supposed to do. Right? Aspiring to these goals is admirable and gives us a sense of great joy and fulfilment. Well... it's not for everyone, and that included me.

My son Luke is my world and means everything to me. No words can express my love for him. He has been and continues to be my rock, my strength, and my legacy. Luke means light, and that's what he's been for me, a lighthouse that has guided me back to the shore when I've been lost at sea in the darkest of storms. He has brought me back from despair many times, and he has been my purpose and reason to carry on. I love you Luke.

There was always something I felt I needed that would fulfil my happiness—whether it was a new car, more money, a new house, or another drink. These beliefs made sure I pursued outward things: if only I had another child, if only I could pay off the mortgage. It was always *if only*. The house was almost paid off, so was the car. I wasn't starving. Things weren't that bad. So what was my problem? Why couldn't I be happy like everyone else? I never felt good enough in the eyes of my wife. Looking back, it was my projection and feelings of self-doubt and inadequacy. I thought life wasn't fair. I was a good man, worked hard, had a great heart, and always did what was needed. I was a good husband, father, son, son-in-law and brother. What was the meaning of all this? Why was my life so screwed up?

The spiritual path kept calling. I was torn between being the family man, and being the seeker wanting to run off to a cave to meditate. I completed Reiki, levels one and two, and hoped my life would start making sense. My confusion, though, thickened into a denser fog and caused my life to unravel faster. I tried everything to break free from the misery that followed me, yet the more I tried... the stronger my feelings of helplessness grew.

I became a vegetarian, and would meditate for hours in front of pictures of the great masters. They say God comes to those who are devoted—that was me. Eager and patient, I waited for a sign, a miracle—something. I begged, played the victim, the bully, the dealmaker, and the manipulator. I tried everything in my power to sway God into taking pity on me. "Please remove me from all this suffering. *If you really love me why do you torture me like this?*" No response. I wasn't even good enough for God. I wrote the songs, 'Wake Me' and 'Surrender' to sway Him. Still nothing. "Fuck *you* and all your bullshit. I've wasted my life searching for something that's not real!"

Once you start on the path of self-realization, you can't go back. I was stuck and very angry about it. "*God, why should the ignorant be allowed to get away with stuff when they haven't put in the work like I have? They haven't meditated for hours every day. They haven't committed to being a vegetarian for seven years. Some don't even believe in you! Why am I getting punished for having integrity?*

*I've done everything right. Why do I have to suffer for being the lone wolf, not fitting in, not being understood?"* There wasn't a day that passed where I didn't question if living like this was worth it. It would have been easier just to pop the red pill and forget about everything. I fell into the trap of spiritual materialism, and believed I had earned the right not to suffer. Ask and ye shall receive? How many more times did I have to knock on His fucking door?

I assumed my knowledge was enough. However, the more I learned, the less I knew. There is a saying, 'God has disappointed many seekers, especially those filled with expectation.' So what else did I have to do? I was losing all patience. Something inside helped me keep keeping on, and continued giving me hope. I went on to learn the ancient art of Indian Head Massage (I.H.M.)—a seven thousand year old healing modality. It addresses the subtle levels of the body, the lymphatic system and pressure points. I was a hairstylist, had learned Reiki and I.H.M. It was the ultimate combination. I could heal anybody!

A hairstylist is always on stage, and it isn't considered professional if they show sadness or that anything is wrong. There were days I pulled off magic, literally. Yet, pressure can build for only so long before it erupts. Mine was a contradiction, an unstable mixture of emotion; abandonment and expectation. Some days the torment was so great, nothing could numb it. One day at work, with a client in my chair, I had a total meltdown. My fuse had blown. My body went numb. My mind became a haze. Like a zombie I lumbered onto the street, my vision blurred by tears. In that moment all that mattered was to find a way off this planet, and out of my body. I'd had enough.

This time it was real, and not fuelled by alcohol or cries for help, as I'd done so many times in the past. I trudged across the street to the library to use the public internet. I typed into the url address bar, 'the best way to commit suicide.' A few options came up, but they were all about prevention. Damn this, it's not what I'm looking for... click... click... where the hell is... yes!

Finally one got my attention. It read something like this: "Are you fed up with life? Do you want to die? Do you hate yourself? Does no one understand your pain?" Each question jacked me up more and more, with a mental 'yes' following each one. This was it. At last someone gets it. They understood my struggle. I felt empowered. Finally I had control over something. I felt exhilarated. This was mine, and no one could take it away from me... click...

The next page left me sobbing uncontrollably. In a pool of tears I was left with a shard of hope that everything was going to be okay. The website was designed to fish you in, emotionally invest you in the content and then turn it around—the perfect bait and switch. I am deeply grateful to the creator of that site. In the past I'd make sure people were around when I attempted to stab myself, or cut my wrists. Was it for attention, or to see if anyone would stop me? Was I worthy enough to stay alive? In the library, it was just me and the computer screen. My decision was final and it was going down that night.

They say you have to hit bottom before you get better. The trouble was, I hit so many low points I didn't know if I'd hit bottom yet. Although it wasn't apparent to me at the time, it was the beginning of the end of my marriage. My divorce was one of the hardest things I have ever done. To this day there are tendrils of remorse that still dangle behind me. I jumped into another relationship six months later, hoping it would be better... only it got worse. It was with a former girlfriend. Call it karma or unfinished business, whatever it was, it started a major healing crisis in my life.

We bought a house together, and with her two boys and my son all under the one roof, it became a freak show. It got really bad, and was much more stressful than my marriage had ever been. Sometimes I couldn't walk due to my bad back, which had plagued me ever since my young promising hockey career had ended at sixteen. It flared up when I was feeling depressed, which was often. My weight and drinking reached it's heaviest. I suffered from trigeminal neuralgia, considered to be one of the most painful afflictions known to medical practice. The condition is a disorder of the fifth cranial (trigeminal) nerve. I was in so much agony that stabbing my face with a knife would seem the best way to lessen the pain.

There were many signs telling me to leave the situation. I knew it was a mistake, but I didn't listen. "This couldn't fail... not again." I had put my heart and soul into renovating that house. Finally after everything was completed I built my coveted recording studio. Then she tells me, "It's over!" I was devastated. The past repeated itself. After four years of hell, I moved out.

Two homes and one investment property were gone, and my financial worth was next to nil. All areas of my life were a mess. As a teenager I invested in a rental property with my parents, aunt and uncle. We had to walk away from it. Every dollar I saved was gone. I might as well have burned it instead.

Forty years of age and what did I have to show for it? Two failed relationships, one marriage, and one common-law. They say it takes ten years to financially get back on your feet after a divorce. I guess it's true about forty being the new twenty! I was overweight, depressed, out of control, and filled with guilt for tearing my son's world apart.

Something had to give. A door had to open. There had to be an intervention, some way to get out of this eternal damnation. I had to do something sensible, for me and my future—anything. With reluctance, I told my father I'd take ownership of the family business. He was probably happy about this, since he was forever telling me I was turning down a goldmine. I was always trying to get away from it. The last thing I wanted was to be a hairstylist, let alone own a salon. My dad was getting older and part of me thought I'd help ease his load. He'd worked hard for most of his life and deserved a break. Twenty-three years later the pattern repeated—do what dad did. Maybe this time my pockets would be lined with wads of cash. Before taking over the business, I set off for a solo three-week hike around Italy—just me and a backpack. It was incredible. I felt alive and with no responsibilities, I was free.

I learned a lot about my parent's motherland, and about myself. It was a different way of life and a peek into another world. It showed me change was possible. Upon my return home, I was overshadowed by melancholy. Life hadn't changed, it was still the same old shit. I'd changed, though, and resolved to live life to the fullest. Owning a business didn't lend itself to that, I owned a salon and all of its responsibilities. Initially it didn't stop me. Although, three years of shenanigans involving booze, strip-joints, strippers, and a plethora of sketchy behaviour almost did me in. Working hungover while running a business wasn't something a forty-five year old man should be doing, especially one who was trying to get his shit together. I wanted to settle down and find my life partner.

How was having a solid woman possible if my heart was closed for business? I was afraid of emotional intimacy. The last thing I wanted was a relationship or to play house again... but, I felt alone.

New books were being read. However, this time they weren't about spirituality, they were on pick up and seduction. I got pretty good at it, even better than when I was five. It was easy to seduce a woman, all it took was one look and I knew it was game on. Today it's different, I don't have a clue anymore, and wouldn't notice if a woman fancied me or not. Could it be that my intentions have changed, or my powers have mysteriously been taken away?

I believe pick-up artists have been terribly hurt in the past by women. I was a flirt, not a 'player,' and what I wanted more than anything was a real soul connection. That's difficult when you're afraid of being vulnerable and lack self-love. So physical intimacy was as far as it went. My fear of getting hurt was the reason why I broke up with everyone I'd ever been with except for one—my former common law girlfriend. She dumped me the first time, then again years later. I got back with her just so I could dump her two weeks later. Ever since, I have treated women unfairly. Was it revenge or to keep safe? I was the jerk women seemed to love, and despised them for it. I hated myself for being that guy. What happened to the compassionate person that would do anything for a woman? Sure, it takes two to tango, but my feelings were compromised, and the guilt weighed heavily on me. I needed to make amends, so I forgave and was forgiven. To this day, I remain friends with these women and am deeply grateful for that. The person who needed forgiveness most, though, still felt unworthy and was full of remorse. He didn't realize the importance of first healing himself. Instead he wrote a list.

Motivational experts tell you to write out a desire list. The theory suggests in order to manifest what you want, you need to have it written down. When the Universe knows what you desire it can get to work on it. Three double-sided pages later, and I had my perfect woman written down—my Twin Flame/ Soulmate. Nothing was spared. Every possible detail had been clarified and my invitation was ready. A chance meeting online, and two and a half years later, she accepted.

The second we laid eyes on each other I knew, she was the one. It was beyond magic and out of this world. I'd never felt attracted to anyone like that before. It was like she came from the heavens, and I couldn't stop looking into her sparkling blue eyes. She matched and exceeded my expectations. I thought, *this stuff really works.* In a matter of months we were looking to buy property and live together. However, something didn't feel right, and one thing I've learned is, if it doesn't feel right, it isn't. To make a long story short, after six months it was over. Patterns quickly revealed themselves. Fear and feelings of unworthiness reared their ugly head. I've been reluctant to make lists ever since, because what we don't know, we don't know.

I'm sure she got more than she bargained for as well. We remain friends to this day.

During the course of my marriage, divorce, and failed attempts at relationships, I visited a few psychics. My reasoning was if I didn't know what to do, they must know better. Since I never visited a therapist I considered them my spiritual shrinks. I hung on to their every word as gospel and stopped listening to my inner guidance. My expectations were high, and caused me to project things to happen a certain way. When they didn't, my self-worth hit the proverbial fan. I'd found a new way to experience rejection. Nevertheless, I still believe a trustworthy Energy Intuitive, psychic or medium can help you find clarity, and show you what doors are open.

*Note: There are a lot of frauds out there, so beware. The way to spot a shyster is by what they promise. No one has the answer to all of your problems. Another tactic they use is the famous, "You have bad luck, and it's because someone has put a curse on you." They will tell you that the only way to remove it is by giving them your money. A true intuitive doesn't need to scare you or to advertise, they are referred by word of mouth. Ultimately, it is best to trust your own intuition.*

I felt a reboot was needed and revisited Reiki levels one and two, and this time did my masters level. I felt ready. Shortly after, I learned an innovative self-healing modality called Sound Reiki®. Sound, intention and tone are used to identify, remove and transmute blocks and limitations. Eventually I earned the recognition of Sound Reiki® Master. The healing world was calling me, and as always there was resistance. I was in the closet. Frank the hairstylist-cum-rock dude clashed with Frank the spiritual guy, who meditated and did Reiki. These worlds were far apart and were set to collide.

Five years after taking over my father's hair salon I got the news—a hand delivered letter from a lawyer. After forty-one years of being at the same location, our family business was ordered to vacate the premises. The building we rented had been sold to make way for a fifty-eight storey condominium. We only had ninety days to vacate. Just three months earlier I lost my mother to cancer at sixty-eight years of age. She had lost her three brothers, younger sister and best friend, all in a short timespan. It felt like my own parents had died. Each of them had helped raise me. My cousins were as close as siblings. So much loss, and all too fast. Life becomes clearer yet more confusing when death visits your loved ones. We question life and ask why we're here, and why we collect things we will eventually have to leave behind? It can change us forever, or until life numbs us back into its repetitive web.

Two years later and I'm here writing to you. I don't know how this story ends, or what's in store. However, I'm excited for whatever is next. We all have a story that hurts, and a life that is less than ideal, but we didn't give up, we persevered. I congratulate you on making it this far. Looking back, everything that's happened has given me insight. I have no regrets, and don't want to change a thing. They've made me into who I am now.

My desire to share what I've learned and experienced in my life is the reason why I wrote this book. I am grateful for every part of it, as all of its pain and joy has brought me to the here and now—to this very moment. It is my intent, that what I've learned can help you in some way, even if it's just to plant the seed of hope.

# CHAPTER TWO

# THE DESCENT

*"Stimulating lies seduce me, building my desire, accumulating ties that bind me, fuelling the burning fire."* *Excerpt from the song 'Wake me' 1993 by Frank Di Genova*

Imagine for a moment, you are an energetic being without a physical body, a soul that is limitless and eternal. You know not of time or space. You are connected to all that is—all is one. What if you were a fragment of singularity that had burst into billions of sparks—a soul that set forth to explore itself? Imagine you and I are expressions of this Divine energy, the source of pure and unconditional Love. Could this just be a concept? Or could it be realized beyond the realm of thought? How would we know of our omnipotence if we had nothing to compare ourselves to? What am I and where do I come from are questions we've been asking since the beginning of time, and no doubt will continue to. Is there a beginning or an end, or is it just an illusion? How do we find the answers to these eternal questions? What if there was a dimension created just for this purpose, a place where we could explore our totality?

What if you wanted to know what an apple was, beyond your mental projection of it? You would have to see, touch, smell and taste it. Only then could you say you've experienced it in its absoluteness. How could this be known unless both you and the apple were in solid form? There is a physical dimension where this is possible. It is called Earth. Energetically, it's a lot denser than what you know, and is surrounded by energy fields that have condensed into solid forms called matter. To enter, you would need to compress your energy, and only then could you experience it. In doing so, your memory would be wiped, all your knowledge forgotten, and nothing but a distant echo would remain.

Since we are one with everything, and time doesn't exist beyond the physical realm, all possible outcomes would be available to us. We could access any one, and in any timeline. You would be at the forefront of experience, exploring your every aspect, idea and creative impulse. Does a voyage like this excite you? Would you choose to enter this realm and explore it? Would you partake in the ultimate journey? Sounds like fun doesn't it? Well, it is supposed to be. Unfortunately, there is a catch, there always is isn't there?

Once you've arrived, it will be very hard to leave, and appears almost impossible. You will be so identified with this new existence, that you'll forget you are limitless and eternal. You'll feel lost and fearful, convinced you've become separated from your infinite source. Gravity and time will distort your sense of being, and your experiences will be perceived in duality in linear sequences. The timeless state you once knew will be gone, and in its place will be limitation. Feelings of being trapped will frustrate you. The longing for something more will constantly gnaw at you. The faint memory of your true nature will forever beckon. Nothing will satisfy you. Your desire to grow will be insatiable and entangle you in its karmic web, so that you're unable to free yourself from its energetic tendrils. The law of attraction will bind you and keep you Earthbound. You will take on new bodies and identities until the desire to go back home prevails.

Often, this journey of creation and self-discovery turns into a painful and reoccurring struggle. The good news is, there is a way out, and off the merry-go-round of lifetimes. You will receive help, the clues will be scattered everywhere. Awakened beings are ready to help show you the way back, and will appear when you ask. You're never alone. Friends always come with you, and are there to help. Sometimes they appear as a lover. Sometimes they're a friend, or enemy. Are you ready to fall asleep? Are you ready for the Ultimate Journey?
Sweetest dreams...

## A RUDE AWAKENING

*"Into a dream I wake, distracted by my senses, clothed by the flesh I take, creating my defences." Excerpt from the song 'Wake Me' 1993 by Frank Di Genova.*

Congratulations on your victory. From the one-hundred million competitors that fought for the grand prize of your mother's egg, you won the ironman of nature where only the healthiest and strongest make it through. There are billions of souls waiting for what you have right now—a body. Are you wasting this opportunity?

You were protected for nine months, and incubated comfortably inside a safe womb, surrounded by warm water. Nourished by your mother, you were connected as one and felt everything she did. Was she looking forward to your birth or dreading it?

The time finally arrives. The water breaks through the dam, and you follow. You are squeezed through a narrow opening, much like dough is from a spaghetti cast. Walls of flesh press against you as you're born into a new unknown world. Intense light painfully blinds your tender eyes, along with a deafening blast of sound that pierces your delicate ears. Your sleeping lungs wake to the cold air. You choke and gasp, forced to breathe for the first time. All you know, is how to cry. You feel cold, afraid, helpless. What a shocking start to your new adventure. This is your first experience, the contrast between pain and pleasure—something that will govern you for the rest of your life.

I had quite the start to my journey. I was born premature at eight months with my stillborn brother by my side. While he didn't make it, I did, at four and a half pounds. Straight into the incubator I went. There I stayed for just under a month. My crying mother stood by, watching helplessly behind the glass wall of the room. She was unable to touch me until I was strong enough to leave my greenhouse. It took many years for me to realize the torment she must have felt. Unable to touch and bond with her baby, and her baby unable to do the same with her—did I really sign up for this?

## INDOCTRINATION

Welcome to Earth... When we arrive, it's ironic that while we're greeted with joy and laughter, we cry with pain. Then in our final moments before death, we are filled with joy, leaving behind the pain and tears felt by our loved ones. We experience trauma by the onslaught of colours, sounds, textures and sensations, that implore us to seek refuge, and comfort. We find ourselves trapped inside our new body, seduced by the senses, and the saturation deepens, slowly dissolving the memory of our celestial origins. Our sense of unity and connection with Divine Source subtly fades, and is replaced by the identification of our new body, surroundings and tribe. We are pliable, trusting, rendered helpless, and rely heavily on our caregivers. They too came into this world, vulnerable, and fully dependant. As the twig is bent, the tree shall grow...

My new tribe gave me a script to follow, one which was passed down from generations. I learned how to speak their language, and assimilate their religion, customs and belief systems. My family history, food preferences and style of dress were moulded over time. I had a name, a family, a culture, and yes, I was part of a tribe. All I had to do was follow their code, and everything would be okay. Being born into and Italian family was awesome. They have great food, a close family connection, and homemade wine. I'm proud of my heritage, but as I got older, other customs and tribes began to interest me.

'All for one and one for all' was the motto used by the characters in Alexandre Duma's book titled, 'The Three Musketeers.' This saying described how a collective group pledge to support one another. The group and each individual abide by each other. Your family and to a lesser extent, ethnicity, have a similar mindset. Flags, sports teams, and national anthems also represent division and uniqueness. We are led to believe 'our' way is better, which further enforces our separation and differences from one another. Race not only divides us, it is our religion, village, town, state, province, and country as well. Does it ever end? How about continent, hemisphere, planet, solar system and beyond?

There is an unwritten rule in most families to follow protocol, it's encouraged and we abide. We are rewarded when we do, and punished when we don't. Sometimes retribution is subtle, at other times it's not. I was surprised to learn the Amish (a traditionalist culture) shun their family and its members if they don't follow their rules and beliefs. My initial reaction to this led me to think it was a bit harsh and archaic. Could this invariably be the case for all families, cultures and society in general? This is true within the caste system of India and in the confines of royalty, and in the hierarchy in politics. Is there no division amongst them? This also affects the working class, that are separated by income levels. Secret clubs, societies, and street gangs require you to prove your allegiance. I was obedient and followed the family's rules, because I wanted to fit in. Thank God I didn't have to make cement shoes or do anything hardcore to prove I was part of my clan. This is probably why mafia movies never appealed to me, except for Goodfellas. The closer I got to my teens, the farther was my desire to conform.

Did you have a strong will? Were you the perfect child? There is always a black sheep in every family. I considered myself the grey sheep. I complied, but inside there was resistance. I felt like an alien living in a world that didn't resonate, and suffered because of it. My mother would often say, "Who are you, where did you come from?" She noticed I was different, as did my father. Whenever I got into deep conversations with my clients, my dad would often say, "He's not my son." In retrospect they were compliments, but at the time they hurt deeply. Sure I was different, but I felt flawed.

## BELIEF SYSTEMS

*"Inventing a million identities, and you try to please them all, protecting these collected memories, the very ones that are gonna make you fall." Excerpt from the song, 'I Can See Right Through You' 1996 by Frank Di Genova*

We are born as empty sponges, and become less absorbant as we get older, sometimes to the point of not being able to absorb any more. Experience teaches, when we touch a hot flame we feel pain, and when we pet a cat we feel pleasure. Everything that meets with our senses becomes a reference point as to how we will model our belief system. Our parents play a huge role early on, as we most often accept what they believe in blind faith. Our friends, relatives, educational systems, and all forms of media later contribute to this. We're all different, and create belief systems based on our unique characteristics.

Are you the type who believes whatever an authority figure says is right? Or do you challenge it? Even if it means being shunned socially? Do you accept what you hear, to fit in, even at the expense of how you feel inside? Are you a follower or a leader? When we challenge an accepted truth, whether it's true or not, we may get attacked. Running with the herd is so much easier than running against it. There are more sheep than there are wolves.

When I was a child, I believed whatever anyone told me. Why would they lie? People who were older had my confidence, as did anyone I perceived who had a higher status than myself. I learned we trust people who we respect and are emotionally attached to. Doctors, specialists, and those considered having authority and expertise in their field are easily trusted. Once upon a time politicians and religious leaders were highly regarded as well. Should they be? Adolf Hitler said, "He alone, who owns the youth, gains the future... give me a child when he's seven and he's mine forever." A despicable quote indeed. However, this demonstrates how essential proper early childhood education is. As a young mind is easily shaped, it's imperative we are aware of what we imprint on their delicate psyche. Parents, musicians, performers, athletes, actors and coaches, have a powerful influence over young impressionable minds.

Are you aware of your behaviour and how it affects the little ones in your life? Children are like baby elephants, easy prey. Did you know an adult elephant can easily pick up a one ton load with his trunk? Have you ever wondered why they don't escape from the confines and abuse in a circus? Trainers bind them to a secure post with a metal chain. Their natural instinct is to try to free themselves. The strong chain holds them back and prevents their attempt to break free. The elephant grows older and believes there's no chance for freedom, even when a weak rope is used instead. The animal has been broken, feels helpless and dejected, and complies when given orders. That same elephant if allowed, could learn how to paint and express itself. There are fourteen known elephants currently painting worldwide. Imagine that, elephants painting with their trucks—incredible. How many of us are broken and bound by invisible chains? How many of us feel free to create and express ourselves?

The Earth was once believed to be flat, and women on their menstrual cycle were considered to be evil and unclean. Santa Claus and the Tooth Fairy are very real to many children around the world. There are people who believe in implausible notions, reinforced by their culture, religion and personal experience. Ironically, it was Easter Monday. The day before, my little niece asked me if I went on an Easter egg hunt. "Yes sweetie, I went to the fridge, found some eggs and made myself an omelette. That silly rabbit didn't do a good job at hiding them." She laughed, yet not as hard as the adults, or myself. I'd actually made myself a frittata that morning.

In the science world, something has to be proven and replicated many times before it's accepted as fact. As new information is discovered some conclusions are challenged and need to be re-evaluated—it's an evolving process. The same can be said for our beliefs. We don't know the things we don't know.

## Building our story:

When my mom and dad fought, which is considered a normal and accepted behaviour in my culture, they really went at it. No one seemed to win. Both were very stubborn and needed to have the last word. Sometimes my dad simply overpowered my mom, not physically but verbally, which eventually broke her to tears, and resulted in my father apologizing. Was it a tactic used by my mother? Or was it genuine? Nevertheless, I learned these two strategies when dealing with conflict: attack, and when that didn't work, play the victim. What have you learned?

The paradox of belief:

We will keep believing something until we find a contrasting element or experience that challenges it. If you're stubborn, there is no way anyone will challenge your beliefs. You'll ignore any alternative possibilities and find more proof to further solidify your conviction. Since we live in a dualistic world anything can be used to support any viewpoint. This is why I don't engage in heavy discussions, or listen to debates on the radio anymore, because with enough information you can defend almost anything. Whatever works for you is fine by me. I would have made a great lawyer, as I'm able to look at both sides equally.

Changing our way of thinking:

Beliefs are thoughts we repeat until they are ingrained into our subconscious mind. When they are charged with feeling they become stronger. Affirmation is a way to imbed new beliefs into our subconscious mind, and is done by repeating a word or words (mantra). These thoughts are like a silent program running automatically in the background. How many unaware commands are we operating on? Are we on autopilot?

If we believe we can or can't do something, we're absolutely right! Our subconscious mind is subjective and doesn't think or reason independently. It obeys the commands it receives from our conscious mind. So, if we want 'that something' we have to believe it's possible. If we don't, it's not. It seems so simple, and it is. The problem is due to a virus in our programming... called doubt.

## EARLY NEEDS

*"Questions unanswered, my feelings rejected. People ignoring me, they turn their heads away." Excerpt from the song 'Alone' 1984 by Frank Di Genova*

Beyond our basic physical needs, such as food, water, and shelter, we have others. Emotional needs are crucial for our development and well-being. We need to feel safe, loved, accepted, understood, and allowed to explore our emotions and express our creativity. Before we chose to incarnate, we didn't have a body to protect. We knew our true nature. Then, we forgot who we are. In a perfect world we'd have awakened parents helping us remember. What fun would that be? We came here to figure it all out, and to have fun doing it. Our life becomes a story, and these are shared from one generation to another, as are rituals and customs. They are absorbed and embedded into our psyche. The way mom and dad were programmed by their parents is often how they will endeavour to pattern us. We are made in their image. DNA chains, karmic legacies and genetic blueprints are inherited from our ancestors. They are passed down from our parents to us, then to our offspring, and so on.

Karmic inheritance precedes us for seven years, and seven after. That's a lot of programming we're up against. Some believe we can change this course by altering the affects of our conditioning, thus potentially changing our genetic coding. Sounds kinda crazy doesn't it? If this is true then it's our responsibility to revise undesirable behavioural patterns, so we don't perpetuate them. Does our conditioning play an ultimate role in who we are?

The age old question, nature versus nurture leaves us asking, are we born this way, or do we behave according to our life experiences? Are we bound by predestined coding in our genes, or can we choose who we want to be in life? I believe it is both.

We often blame our parents for things they did to us growing up, for not understanding, or for not showing up. I'm sure they did the best they could. Life doesn't come with instructions, especially on parenting. They had to wing it. Blaming them is pointless, and only complicates life, creating cyclical patterns which are often passed down. Being a parent myself, one thing I've realized is the instinctual need for a parent to protect their child, as both my parents did for me. Sometimes that supervision can be lacking, objective, or excessive, and is brought on by being over cautious or negligent.

My mother hated germs and was vocal about it when I touched stuff I wasn't supposed to. I can still hear her gross yuck sounds when I see something disgusting. She was proud of her home and liked to keep it extra clean. I didn't share her views. Still, I respected her and her house, and did my best to keep it spotless. I remember making my friends walk along the edges of the hallway so their sweaty socks didn't make footmarks on the unblemished ceramic floor. My friends and I often skipped class to drink beer in our basement kitchen. We would take the table outside and hose it down so she wouldn't whiff the eau D'Molson Canadian. I inherited her keen sense of smell.

I often protested we were living in a museum, and normal people didn't live like we did. "Do what you want in your own house," she countered. I'd yell back, "Oh ya, when I buy a house, I'm gonna shit on my kitchen floor and you can't clean it up!"

My bedroom became my safe haven, a place to kick back and relax; that was until she barged in unannounced and started cleaning my room shouting, "This is a pig-style." Only later did I learn it was called a pig-sty. Mom, I'm sure you're laughing about this.

My father protected me in a different way. He'd shield me from experiencing all hardships, completely unaware he was setting me up to fail. He would do everything for me, even build my kite and crash it before I got a chance to fly it. It was a WW1 Fokker Dr. 1 Triplane, made from strips of wood, glue and paper. I had to wait until he came home from work to watch him make it, which took several weeks to build. He did everything for me, maybe so I wouldn't fuck up. Perhaps he was afraid to lose me again. He lost my brother and my mother during her labour. He was told his *only* son was stillborn and he was losing his wife. Five blood transfusions later and the surprising news arrived that there was another—a twin—brought us both back to him. Years later, another scare loomed, as a life threatening bout of appendicitis left me with only hours to live.

It's common for a child and young teenager to feel responsible for their parents happiness. I wanted to make mine proud, and I blamed myself when they weren't. Years later I learned it had nothing to do with me; we all have our own shit to deal with. We want to earn our parents love and acceptance. I'm sure they anticipate ours too. Sometimes, though, they don't know how to show it. The basic needs required to nurture a child's emotional development cannot be bought or sourced out. Spoiling them with money, luxury and material comforts will never replace giving them the attention and acceptance they need. Proper nurturing allows a child to grow into a well-adjusted and emotionally mature adult. Money and luxury can be absent, but if love and acceptance is, shit will eventually hit the fan.

Are you an emotionally available person? Or, have you checked out? Can you give others their space, be present, and listen without imposition or judgment? When we take responsibility for our actions, we stop blaming others. If we weren't criticized as a child, we wouldn't need to judge others, or ourselves. In a perfect world, emotional maturity would be way more common than it is.

When we don't *get* what we need, these unfulfilled desires create feelings of unworthiness and not being good enough. We lose the ability to trust and feel safe, to love and be loved. Walls are created to protect ourselves from any further hurt. These literal blocks limit and distort our perception. We can become invisible, preferring to remain hidden, get angry and lash out. Sometimes we try to control the outcome by closing off and resisting, by raising our shield and drawing our swords.

If our parents were unable to support our needs, who 'did' we turn to? Was it our children, family, friends, teachers, coaches, coworkers? Maybe it was a romantic partner? Unfortunately, everyone will eventually fail us, because they have their own crap to deal with and are incapable of dealing with ours. Ultimately, we lose faith and trust in people altogether. So where do we go from there? Do we seek unconditional love from a dog, or companionship from a cat? I deepened my relationships with food, alcohol, sex, and drugs. Predictably, these didn't work either.

How many of us still crave the approval of our parents? Are they still alive to make amends? Even if they are, there's no guarantee that chance will ever present itself. Pride, fear and not knowing how, may get in the way. Sometimes it takes a life-changing event to bury the hatchet. I was blessed to have the opportunity to make peace with my mother. I'm forever grateful. She spent over a month in palliative care, which gave me time to resolve my issues. I got to know who she really was beyond her role as my mom, and learned she was a great woman. I realized something profound. Beneath everyone's exterior, they are vulnerable no matter what roles they play or how they appear to be. I feel gifted that I was given this opportunity, and remain forever grateful. The experience of holding her hand until her last breath, gave me strength and wisdom to understand and honour her unconditionally. I felt her struggle and undying love for me as she slipped away. It was the most beautiful experience. There was no guilt or anger, only joy and gratitude. My father and I have started to make amends too. Since her death we both realize that being right no longer matters. Our parents are our greatest teachers, and no matter how many years of spiritual work we do, they know how to push our buttons with skill and ease. Allow them. They will uncover every wound in need of healing.

What we expect in a romantic partner is largely influenced by our parents. My mom always spoke her mind to my father. It's not surprising then, that I attracted similar traits in my former wife. I would act just like my father when confronted with similar circumstances. This isn't a given by any means. We model what we see growing up. I believe a male's father is his role model for how to treat women, and how they allow them to be treated in return. A female models her mother in the same way. Sometimes these templates show us what not to do.

What if the programming of our parents was corrupted? Wouldn't that distort our perspective and affect how we treat our partners and children? I said, "I'd never be like my parents," but the older I got, the more I noticed similar characteristics come to the surface. We are not our parents. Their conditioning may have become our default settings. However, being mindful resets them. If you find yourself becoming just like your mom or dad, maybe you're trying too hard not to become them. What you resist becomes your reality. Instead of reacting with defence or attack, due to old programming, be mindful and treat others as you want to be treated.

Looking back on your childhood, are you aware of anything your mother or father did that made you feel sad, or angry? Are you still carrying around any wounds and resentments? If you have the inclination, get out a piece of paper and write down your answers to these questions.

Ask yourself:

- *Have I ever felt judged, criticized or ridiculed?*
- *Was I ever made to feel stupid or not good enough?*
- *Did I ever let them down, or have they ever let me down?*
- *Could I trust my parents, and family members, did they lie to me?*
- *Did they pay attention to me or did they ignore me?*
- *Was I allowed to express myself: emotionally, verbally, creatively?*
- *Did I feel they loved me enough?*

There will always be something we can blame our parents for—trivial or not. Some we can let go of, while others we bury deep inside. It would be easier just to forget it all, but we can't. We trusted these people, and bought into everything they said. We relied on them. These false perceptions may have become our core beliefs, either limiting or empowering us. They are just stories we keep repeating, over and over, that we allow to control our lives. If I told you a funny joke you would probably laugh. If I repeated it, you would no doubt laugh again, but not as much. What if I kept saying the same joke over and over? Would it still be funny? Most likely not. You'd think I was a bit crazy. So if we stop laughing after we've heard the same joke over and over, why do we keep crying over the same sad story we keep telling?

*Dear Mom and Dad,*

*You let me down, hurt my feelings, and caused me to feel inadequate and worthless. I bet you didn't know I used to inflict blows to my face with a closed fist, to punish myself. Did you know the reason why I drank myself stupid as a teenager? Because I hated myself. You spoiled me rotten and I resented it, just as much as I loved it. You didn't have a clue what I really needed. I wanted you to understand me. Yes, I knew you loved me, but you didn't understand I needed emotional support. I was vulnerable. You didn't know my struggle, what I endured, why I had to keep it all inside. You're my parents, why didn't you know?*

*P.S.*

*I want to thank you so very much for everything you did for me. I forgive you for all the things I thought were unfair. I am grateful for the courage you had in doing the best you could, when you didn't know any other way. I am thankful for carrying me when I couldn't walk, and for protecting me when I was in danger, when I didn't know any better. Please forgive me when I lashed out at you in anger, and for pulling me back when I wanted to jump. I am indebted to you for being the perfect parents. You have allowed me to grow the way I needed to. You've afforded me the perfect conditions to learn everything I came here to learn.*

*Deepest Gratitude,*

*Frankey*

# CHAPTER THREE

# HYPNOSIS &
# ENSLAVEMENT

*"You'll only fool people like you, acting out your imagined play. Living life always the same way through, in the same old lame mechanical way." Excerpt from the song 'I Can See Right Through You' 1996 by Frank Di Genova"*

Since the early seventies, my father had Playboy magazines delivered monthly to the salon. You can imagine the collection. My prerequisites for the perfect woman were honed by the hundreds of bunnies that crossed my eyes. Along with my once porn addiction, this jaded my reality of what a real woman was supposed to look like. It took me many years to realize that those types of women didn't exist. There were only so many pictorials to salivate over before one became bored. One day I found an article—it blew me away. It was about how the African government thwarted U.S. attempts at food and medical relief from its own people. Care packages were dropped via aircraft close to the villages; the African military were ordered to intercept them before the villagers got to them. That definitely made me lose my erection. Playboy might be an entertainment magazine for men, yet it really had good articles.

The write-up got me thinking, *how and why would any government want to keep their people down?* Here in Canada our Aboriginals live on reserves. The living conditions are less than ideal, and the quality of the water is inadequate. Some will argue internal problems are keeping these people down in status. What about the ghettos and shantytowns of the world? Do they breed destitution? The problems are complex and so are the solutions; the dichotomy continues, and not only affects the aforementioned.

Could it be possible, that what I read in Playboy is happening on a larger scale? Could we be controlled, kept asleep, and led to believe we are free? I'm sure deep down you feel something is off, not quite right, but you can't put your finger on it. It appears the elite have all the money while the rest struggle to get by. The more money we make, the more it's taken away by tax. Cancer and disease are claiming more of our loved ones, and gets worse each day. Then there's global warming, natural disasters and deforestation. What the hell is going on? Maybe there is something happening. Perhaps it's not just on a global level. What if it's so insidious it's happening right under your nose?

## HYPNOSIS & OPPRESSION

Hypnosis is an induced state of consciousness in which a person appears to lose their power of voluntary action, and is very susceptible to suggestions. Therapeutically, it can be used to lose weight, quit smoking, or, to stop an undesired behaviour. These are a few examples. What concerns me, is the trance state we all seem to be under, conjured by our media and technology. Are we also oppressed by the same forces that are distracting us?

We have no clue how powerful we are. Instead we choose to stay asleep. Has it ever occurred to you that we could be under a mass hypnosis that keeps us distracted from realizing our Divinity? Could our mind and sensory perceptions be what keep us locked in a virtual prison? Do you remember the baby elephant? What if we were all incarcerated in a pseudo-jail, fabricated to appear like we were free? This would be an ultimate mind fuck, where we're both the inmates and the guards policing each other so we don't escape. God forbid anyone mention we live in such a penitentiary. You'd be ridiculed, accused of being a jail breaker, an ex-con who challenges the system. For those who don't back down, their fate is not as forgiving. Some get burned at the stake, others tortured, or even crucified. If you believe paying bills, working forty-plus hours per week as a debt-slave is normal, then you may be under a spell. As long as we are pacified, and kept distracted everything is okay. As long as we continue to purchase the products they tell us to buy, the system keeps working. Imagine how many corporations would go out of business if we accepted ourselves just the way we are?

## SELF-WORTH

Having low self-esteem may be a direct result of our upbringing. It may be instilled by our family, friends, educators or employers. Whatever the case, seeking approval from another is giving away our power. Our need to fit in makes us vulnerable and easy to influence. With self-assurance, validation isn't needed from anyone, and is internal, unconditional self-acceptance. Confidence is born by loving and accepting ourselves unconditionally, not from what others think. Unfortunately, that's not the case when we're young. We worry about what others think, and the older we get, the less we care. Although, not always.

Early in my career I used to charge certain clients less for their hair, in an attempt to win them over. Sometimes I felt sorry for them and gave them a discount. At other times it was more than that. I once met an attractive woman in a club, and gave her my business card. She called a few weeks later to book an appointment. After her hair was done, she thanked me and proceeded straight for the door. It turned out, I told her I'd give her a free haircut. So much for liquid courage! There were other times I gave my services for free. You'd think I would have learned. I have. Now, whenever I do hair, a healing or consult, I do with love and without ego. Money is simply energy, and represents the exchange of worth. My clients receive value and one hundred percent dedication, and in return they show me their appreciation by paying me for it. People who want deals have no appreciation for others nor themselves.

Society has a way of duping us into believing we need to follow and conform. Who is shepherding the herd? Where is it being led? Trying to resist is difficult, especially when you know the herd is heading for the cliff. It's hard to go against the flow. Everyone is wearing a mask, afraid of being called out. People buy into the facade and act like they have it all together.

The hair business is notorious for this. It's part of the fashion machine, the Pied-Piper of insecure mice. Fashion comes and goes, sometimes lasting only a few weeks. In its wake, hordes of servants scurry to keep up. Pop stars and actors all have their fifteen minutes of fame, then get spat out and replaced by the next one. It staggers me what people do to their body to appear beautiful. Wouldn't it be easier to be authentic, and not worry about what others think? Too many people try to outdo each other, jealous and competitive, no one wins this game. Authentic beauty radiates from within. It's eternal and forever. Physical beauty is fleeting like the cherry blossom.

The ego-mind can be convinced to accept a promise, or future reward. All that's needed is your patience and trust. If you do what they say: work harder, pay your dues and suffer just a bit more, you'll earn the prize. The promise is a tactic used by master manipulators who get you to buy in. Obey and you will enter heaven. Vote for us and we'll lower your taxes. How does an abusive partner get away with physically and emotionally hurting you? What does a scam artist promise you so you'll give them your money to invest in their get rich quick scheme? All you have to do is trust them, and hope your greed knows best. Lack of self-worth, greed, and the need for approval makes us susceptible to manipulation.

## SENSE BOUND

Our mind and corporeal senses are the faculties we use to interpret and explore this physical world. They're also what binds us to it. Most people are unaware that other spectrums could exist beyond what our physical senses perceive. Why would one think otherwise, when all we can grasp is a fragment of a larger unknown? Do you have to see something in order to believe it? Do you sense there is something more? Have you ever thought about someone and suddenly the phone rings (or messages) and it's them? Ever had a gut feeling about something that ended up being right, but you didn't listen? I'm sure you've been aware of other signs, and passed them off as coincidence. Why do we try rationalizing these events? Are we afraid of opening Pandora's box? Maybe it's the fear of losing control, our identity, or feeling as though we have to give up our core beliefs. Sometimes ignorance is bliss. Regardless, it's the very thing that keeps us bound to a system we can be totally oblivious to.

## MY HYPNOSIS

I wasn't chained to a desk, however, I was to a job. I had a love-hate relationship with it. I used to commute three hours everyday. It didn't matter if it was by train or by car, the delay was the same. The clogged traffic and train delays always left me feeling helpless, trapped, and unable to move. Rush-hour was indifferent to my clients who waited for me at work, and at home. The stress of working two jobs took its toll on me. When Luke was born, my then wife and I decided she would stay home for his benefit. My decision was hastened when the potential babysitter we were interviewing accidentally dropped him, right in front of us. It took a bit of convincing for his mom to agree, as she held a good job. This also meant we'd take a financial hit.

I would work all day and sometimes miss lunch. Me without food was not a good thing. After a long and stressful day, I'd be on that train heading home to more clients. My plan was to slowly build a clientele base close to where I lived, avoid the long commute downtown, and spend more time with my family. My former wife worked as an aerobics instructor and would leave to teach when I got home. In a perfect world I'd arrive home on time, she'd leave, and I'd do a client while my son was either watching me or playing. The timing was crucial, and didn't always play fair. My father was my boss, my boss was my father. Capisce? We didn't get along at the best of times, so you can imagine how stressful it was just being at work.

Like most of us in the rat race, we know how draining it can be. At times my stress was unbearable. Why was life so hard? Why did it feel like I was on a hamster wheel going nowhere fast? I felt like I was dying. Life wasn't fun. In actual fact, it sucked. I did everything right, worked hard, and cared for others, yet I felt like a piece of unworthy crap—defeated. What was I doing wrong? Fuck my life and all the assholes who gave more of a damn about money than people. I wasn't going to be that guy. It wasn't in my nature. Why did I suffer for having integrity and morals? To help me cope, I became good friends with vodka and food. We didn't want Luke to become a television zombie, so we cancelled our cable. Smartphones and Facebook hadn't been invented, or I'd have been having an affair with them too. My spiritual practices were on hold. Why bother? God didn't seem to want to help me anyway.

If there was a way to contact that version of myself I'd tell him a few things. Maybe he exists, somewhere within me, still holding onto the hurt, reminding me of how it used to be. "I hate to break it you buddy, but we don't live in a utopian world, nor will it ever be. You are smart enough, you just don't know the game. When you figure it out you'll stop struggling. There are greedy power-hungry individuals not caring about your best interests. They want you to stay docile and unquestioning, so you keep feeding the system they created. We're all given just enough to get by, so we don't revolt and start a revolution. They've led us to believe we're not capable of fighting back. Stop being their slave. Stop rowing and get off their ship.

## MASS HYPNOSIS

I wonder how much longer we can last under this system. Not long ago the family unit was stronger, and one provider was enough to support it. Now it takes two incomes, or one very good one. Has our greed replaced the enjoyment of the simple things in life? Or does everything just cost too much? Families are stressed and breaking apart. Both parents need to work, which leaves their children to the system to raise them. Tv, tablets, internet, and video games pose as trusted babysitters. These *things* can't be fully monitored. Children are stuck indoors, hypnotized by what's on the screen. Shared family dinners are rare as everyone's schedules are different. We live with so much fear that we don't let our kids play outside anymore. We arrange supervised playdates and put helmets on our kids so they can brush their teeth. No one has the time to cook wholesome food. Instead, we opt for fast and convenient, which is often less healthy. Stress has never been higher. We've become impatient, unhealthy, and barely cope because of it. How many of us use alcohol, drugs and stimulants, such as coffee to get by? Children are no better. They're jacked up on sugar, and prescribed medication.

As long as we're distracted we won't question how we really feel. The less we know of what's really going on, the better. We are blasted with world news, conflict in the Middle East, who's banging who in Hollywood, and smut in the tabloids, binge tv watching, sports, political smokescreens, and the music scene have all been designed to keep us distracted. We are filled with useless information that doesn't mean shit. Luke was undertaking Business Marketing in college and told me we are subjected to over one thousand ads each day. That's a lot of information coming at us. It was a lot different even fifteen years ago, with less technology available. Is what we're absorbing also influencing our food choices, the clothes we buy, and the car we drive? Are we being led to believe our safety is in jeopardy, that we need to fear an enemy, and give up our rights for protection? Who is the enemy we need to be protected from?

## GOVERNMENT

Does our vote really count? Do we have the power to actually affect change?

In Canada, we have a parliamentary system, where the candidates for our Prime Minster are not directly elected by voters. We get to choose which one we like, but we don't get to select the candidate. The establishment puts them in place. I'm not up on my American politics, but isn't it the same, where only a few states allow voters to pick a candidate? What I find interesting is both Canada and the U.S. have us choose between the red and blue parties. When we get upset at one, we can vote for another preselected one, and the game keeps on going.

Have you ever thought the left and right wing may belong to the same bird? We are under the illusion we have a choice, but we don't. The characters change and the story stays the same. It doesn't matter if you pick heads or tails, it's the same coin. Has anything really changed historically with the government? They all promise reform, then blame the previous regime for the mess they assured us they'd fix—it's impossible. The original function of the government was to serve its people. Somehow, this translation got lost. Instead they take our money, live off the hog and start wars, and we get to pay for their irresponsible spending and screw ups. No problem, just bill the people, and raise their taxes.

## EDUCATION

My son always looked at things differently. He thought for himself and I encouraged that. Luke struggled in grade school, and I thought this was caused by the trauma of my divorce. One night he was at my place and asked me to help him with his homework. He was stuck on an assignment. I could tell he was very frustrated. "What's wrong Luke?" "Dad, I can't figure this out. It doesn't make sense." We both looked at the problem and I asked how the teacher explained it in class. "I don't remember, but it doesn't make sense." I asked him the same question and got the same answer. "Okay Luke, let's look at the front of the lesson in the workbook. There is always an example." After reading a few words, it hit me. It was an epiphany. "Luke, I struggled in school too. I get it now."

He looked at me and must have wondered what was going on in my head. "You can't figure this out because it's not common sense... it doesn't apply to real life." He was trying to figure out the problem rationally. "From now on you're going to give them what they want, garbage in... garbage out, no questions. Use your mind when you're out of class, in real life." It may have sounded harsh, but since that pivotal moment his grades climbed over thirty percent and were sustained. If only someone had told *me* this at his age, I wouldn't have been so hard on myself. I am in no way putting any teachers down. There are members in my family and circle of friends who are teachers, and I respect them. They deal with a lot of stress and politics that I wouldn't be able to take. Teacher or not, we are all part of the system—cogs in the machine.

Pink Floyd was never my favourite band, but they were on to something when they created their album, 'The Wall'. Only now can I appreciate their music. The educational system teaches us to memorize, repeat and regurgitate what we're taught. We are trained to memorize curriculums instead of being allowed to think and use our creativity. I was shocked to learn from my little niece that cursive writing isn't taught anymore, and is now considered art. As a result, our creativity is being stifled. No one fails anymore. Our children are being homogenized. This type of training seems like it's preparing children to become unquestioning robots—drones to feed the elite. The aristocrats appear to be handpicking and hobnobbing their own, privy to the luxury of higher education and knowledge. The rest have to work for it.

## RELIGION

What better way to make people conform than to convince them they are sinners, and they will burn in hell if they don't obey? I was taught, 'the meek shall inherit the earth, and that money is the root of all evil'. Before receiving communion I had to say, "Lord I am not worthy to receive you but only say the word and I shall be healed." God forbid if I did feel worthy, it would've been the work of the devil. Ironically, this came from people who sat on golden thrones in front of fancy alters, in a place of worship where there were stained glass windows and expensive furniture. Sure I bought into it. It was intimidating.

One day, my father saw our parish priest downtown. He wore a leather jacket, and walked arm in arm with two beautiful women at his side, both their arms laced around his. When he recognized my father, he pretended he didn't know him, and kept walking. He drove a red Camero and wore leather racing gloves. Damn, I should have been a priest. How often are we told to have patience, and times are tough, all we need is faith? We go to church to find the answers, when in fact it's part of the problem. As you can tell by now, I'm no longer religious. However, I am devoted to my search for Divinity and truth. In no way is it my intention to discourage religion or bash any-ones faith.

## THE MONEY TRAP

Money is the biggest form of slavery we have. Granted, we need it to live. But the way it's presently structured is a trap. The money system is set up so that the majority can't be rich, unless they find a way, shady or not, to escape. Historically, different items were used to trade goods and services, such as livestock, gems, and precious metals. At one point salt, was highly valued and used as the standard form of exchange. The word *salary* and the phrase *worth his salt*, were derived from the word *salt*. Pelts, leather, and coffee were other items used for trade, until gold became the standard for the world.

You would go to the bank and deposit your gold, and receive a banknote representing its value. Your banknote (money) could then be used to buy things. You didn't need to lug around your gold, or trade your chicken for a haircut. At any time, you could go to the bank and get your gold back with promissory notes. In 1933 it all changed. The Gold Act Reserve made it illegal to own or trade gold, and it had to be given to the Treasury. In 1971 money was taken off the old standard and became fiat (currency), which meant it wasn't tied to anything. Not many know the government isn't responsible for printing money—private companies do that. I'm not going to get into the whole racket. It's in-depth and I want to keep it simple.

Let's say you want to buy a house. You'll need a loan, so you go to a bank and borrow the money. Once upon a time, they would lend you the equivalent of how much gold was in their vault. Nowadays, the bank hardly has any money, let alone gold. This is where it gets really fucked up. With just a few keystrokes, they can magically create any amount you ask, from thin air. Now you are on the hook to repay them over three times the value of your loan, which isn't real. They're charging you interest on invisible money. If you don't pay, they will take your house. It's criminal. The bank now owns twenty-five or more years of your hard labour, which is the time you spend away from your family, friends and enjoyment of life. You are a slave, and The Man owns you. Who's going to put these Banksters in jail?

In 2015-2016 Iceland said enough and jailed them all. So the next time you think you own your house, think again. Even if your mortgage is paid off, you still don't own your house. Why? Try not paying property taxes and see what happens. The government has the power to take it away from you too. While we are at it, what about your body? Won't you have to give that back one day too?

I quickly learned how The Man can take your money when I owned my business. There were costs such as the rent, payroll, business licence, qualification licence, insurance, utilities, bank fees, point of sale fees, harmonized tax, income tax, lawyer fees, accounting fees, supplies—I could go on. The disparity of what I earned and took home was unbelievable. I thought, "Who the fuck am I working for?" It sure the hell wasn't me. To scrape by I thought I had to endure all that stress! Most of us are leveraged beyond our means, in debt and paying insane interest rates. Consider getting out of debt, pay off all loans and stop using credit cards and lines of credit. If you can't, then you are living beyond your means and need to reassess your lifestyle.

## NEED VS WANT

When Luke was little, I created a game. It was to teach him the difference between needs and wants. We called it the need and want game. I would ask him if certain things were something we needed or wanted. After he got really good at the basics, I would make the game harder. He got so good at it he was asking me what the differences were. The purpose of the game wasn't to limit him in anyway, it was to show him the difference between what was necessary and what wasn't. I taught him that *things* don't make us happy; happiness is an inside job. If we want something, it's for the experience it gives us, not to keep score. We both share a love for Lamborghinis. My desire to own one has subsided, while his still burns. On his nineteenth birthday, my present was a few laps around the track in his dream car, the Gallardo. I thought if he drove one that'd be enough—no! One day he will pull up in my driveway in a Lambo, and when he does, the deal is that I'll take it for a spin.

## GREED

Greed is wanting more than is required, even after all your needs have been met. It separates us from others, as having more can make us feel superior. Greed is an insatiable pit of desire, there's never enough. We think we need more to be happy, to feel complete, and the corporations know and prey on this. We put so much value on things that they are coveted, stolen, and withheld. Try taking something away from a child, and see what happens. Whenever something is taken from a child (they think they own everything) they cry, "Mine!" They will fight and claw until they get it back. Yet, as soon as they do, they don't care for it anymore. We want what we don't have, and when we have it, we don't want it anymore. Human nature.

A drunk found a magic lamp on the street, rubbed it and a genie came out. The drunk was granted three wishes. "I want a big glass of beer that is always refilled when I've finished it." Poof! It appears in his hand. He downs it all (every last drop) and it magically refills. He drank three more glasses and it kept refilling. "What is your next wish?" the genie asked. "Give me two more, exactly the same."

## CONTROL

Why are natural ways of treating pain and disease not supported by the pharmaceutical industry? It wouldn't have anything to do with the hundreds of billions of dollars a year they make in profit would it? Is our food being controlled by engineered seeds that don't regerminate? Have we become dependent on the system to feed us? If shit hits the fan and our food industry is completely wiped out (or destroyed), would you know how to grow your own food? Consumerism is dependant on us to consume. Our senses are highjacked, and we become addicted. Our fear is their food. We give away our power in exchange for the security they falsely promise us, so we can feel we belong in their synthetic world.

# CHAPTER FOUR

# THE FALSE SELF

*"If you run away I will find you, devour your soul. Stop your foolish battles, you'll never win with me." Excerpt from a previous version of the song 'Fear' 1991 by Frank Di Genova*

The *ego* is structured by the mind, emotions, and five senses. It's a fabricated indentity which deceives us into believing it's only the body. Our soul knows we're all connected as one: to the Earth, the stars, and the totality of the Universe. The ego is an imposter posing as you, and uses the alias 'I'. There is no you or me. There is no separation. Even now as you read this, you may feel resistance to accepting it.

## EGO

Many spiritual modalities tell us we must destroy the ego for our liberation. However, this is impossible and altogether irresponsible. We need it. Our ego is necessary, not only to perform daily tasks, but to aspire to become a greater person. It ties our shoes, combs our hair, and tells us we need to shower. Unfortunately, the slave has become the master, and the servant has turned rogue, abusing its power.

As our consciousness expands, our ego resists and tries to stop the process. It can't accept the new reality we've awakened to. It's afraid of change and addicted to the old one. Eventually when the ego feels safe, it will integrate, but not without kicking and screaming. I remember my first day of school, and the fear I had. By the end of the day I didn't want to leave. The coward turns into a king, then back into the coward. Our false self deceives us by giving the impression it doesn't exist. But every adversary has a weakness, and this rival has many. It hides like a wizard behind the curtain of our mind, afraid of being seen, frantically working the levers inside our cerebral control room. Once you notice, you realize it's only a fearful child, who feels easily threatened and is quick to defend. The ego is very insecure, and needs constant praise and reassurance. When the light of unconditional love is present, the ego disappears along with the shadow.

The ego needs to feel superior, stronger, faster and bigger than others. Who remembers the game 'king of the hill,' where the object was to stay at the top of a hill, while others tried to push you off? "I'm the king of the castle and you're the dirty rascal." The king is a construct of the mind, established in time. It can't exist in a timeless state. The mind triggers our emotions in response to perceptions based on sequential events. Emotions such as guilt, shame and regret, are distilled from past experiences. While anxiety and fear are anticipated projections from an unknown future. When we're fully present in a *now* moment the mind becomes idle and does not participate. The only control the mind-ego has over us, is fear. And since fear cannot exist when we are present, it's powerless. The false self believes death and disease only happens to other people. It's invincible and impervious to everything. The moment something arises that challenges this notion, it collapses and pleads, "Why me? What did I do to deserve this?"

## OUT OF YOUR MIND

The function of the mind is to think, organize, decide, and formulate. Like the ego, it's an essential tool. Once again, when the servant becomes the master, and the inmates take over the asylum, all hell breaks loose. Buddha described the human mind as being filled with drunken monkeys, all jumping around causing trouble, and yelling for attention. Fear is the loudest monkey, and constantly sounds the alarm for what could go wrong.

We believe thinking is a good thing. Nothing can be further from the truth. Excessive mental-chatter is the biggest way we distract ourselves. Silence is the mind's enemy, much like the timeless now is to the ego. Both are their assassins. Stillness is the portal through which we experience ourselves as infinite beings, connected to all things. Neurotic thinking is a feeble attempt to control a projected outcome, and is one of many possibilities that hasn't happened.

If one was to calculate the algorithm and mechanics of how a bird flies, they'd be busy and distracted. Does the bird that elegantly flies think of what it's doing? Let the mind do its job when needed. Embrace and enjoy the moment, and let your heart inspire you. Get out of your head, and feel, act and do from the heart. Look at the flower and enjoy its beauty. Don't analyze it, because when you do, it stops being beautiful. I used to do that with women, picking out every flaw, and every imperfection. Go by how it makes you feel. Here's a random thought, silent and listen have the same letters. See, my mind just wondered off. Oh yes, the beautiful flower.

## FEAR

*"Your strength starts to crumble, your body starts to shake, sounding like a drum you feel your heart pound and quake."*
*Excerpt from the song 'Fear' by Frank Di Genova 1992*

Fear is the mother all of negative emotions—food for the ego. When we stop allowing it and its offspring to control us, it's powerless. From a spiritual perspective, fear is the opposite of love, or the absence of it. Love is the light, and fear is the darkness. Our ancestors relied heavily on this emotion, because it was necessary for their safety. Our lizard brain produces a fight or flight response, and is essential when we feel threatened. Prehistoric animals are no longer after our heads, so we have less to fear. Modern day perils like the stock market and public speaking have taken its place, and trigger a similar response. With less to worry about we've started focusing on other things, like our individuality and getting ahead in life.

Aside from our inborn fears, such as falling, being startled by loud sounds, experiencing death, and so forth, most of what we fear is simply a mental projection. Children might be afraid of the boogie man in the closet, or the monster hidden under the bed. The alien robot at the top of the stairs used to scare the shit out of me. Even now when I dangle my hand over the edge of the bed at night, it gives me the creeps. What if something grabbed my hand? Fear is responsible for keeping us small and powerless. To break free from this illusory grasp sets us free.

The best way to overcome it is to embrace it, feel the exhilaration of it and move through it. Sometimes it's a warning. So take heed, your higher self may be trying to protect you. A powerful technique for dissolving fear is to allow it to surface and watch it pass. This also works for lessening mental and physical pain. In chapter eleven I share techniques that can help with physical and emotional discomfort.

The cerebrum has three facets: the Reptilian, the Limbic and the Neo-Cortex. Evolving past fear requires the transcendence of our reptilian brain, the part that is responsible for lust, aggression, worship, greed and the need to dominate. The limbic area emerged from the mammal kingdom, and is responsible for our feelings and emotions. As we evolve, we transcend from a primal-fear based consciousness, to an emotional one, then finally to an omnipotent one. My intent with this book, and the next step of our evolution, is to tap into the Neo-Cortex. This area is our super brain, and researchers say it has unlimited potential. This could be the eighty to ninety percent that hasn't been tapped into yet. I wonder if Neo from the movie The Matrix was symbolically named after the Neo-Cortex.

Do you have a fear that immobilizes or prevents you from living a fuller life? Do you know where it came from? A parent? A friend? Or was it genetically passed down? Is the media fuelling fear, keeping our vibration low and suppressed? What are you really afraid of? Failure? Success? Or both?

## ANGER

Anger comes from wanting something we don't have, or from an expectation that didn't happen. Do you get angry when something bad happens to you or a loved one? Do you lash out and blame the situation or person? Anger is a destructive force. It skews our thinking and eventually weakens our health. It must be tamed if we are to live a more peaceful life. Fire against fire doesn't defuse rage, it only strengthens it, and fuels the clash. Anger is a wild and uncontrollable beast—it's vengeful. When someone is in a heated rage, Indian yogis recommend they take a cold shower to literally cool off.

Anger isn't necessarily bad, if it's expressed properly. It can be used to motivate and inspire others into action; although, only when we have total command over it. I didn't. It had the best of me for a longtime. I was easily possessed, undisciplined, and triggered. I used to punch holes in walls, throw and break things, and yell at the top of my lungs. Thankfully, they're only distant memories. The fire has quelled, and it takes a lot to trigger me now. One time I nearly laid a fist to my former wife's head. My rage and strength would have probably killed her with one blow. I'd never hit a woman and wasn't going to start. Instead, my fist hit our bed's wooden headboard. The crushed knuckles were enough to stop me from a repeat performance.

When anger is uncontrolled it's dangerous. It can be like riding a motorcycle for the first time. That happened to me with my friend's powerful Ninja motorcycle. It was my first time on a steel horse. I cranked the throttle, the bike lurched forward, and I lost control. My friend was grateful for the nearby grass, where I laid his bike down, not so gently. Once you have control over the anger, it no longer commands you and can be used in a more positive way.

How does hate differ from anger? The difference between them is the intensity and duration. Hate is deeper and more sustained, and is carried longer. Anger is more of a response, while hate is the fear of being dominated. Violence is the result of hate and is the reaction to feeling our survival is in question. Jealousy is lower on the intensity scale, and is the result of feeling beaten or inadequate. Feelings of being hurt or losing something we love leads to rejection. Hate is powerful, in that whatever you hate, you will attract to yourself—as is with all emotions.

## GUILT

Feelings of guilt arise when we betray our moral code, or fail to keep a promise. It happens when we keep giving in to a bad habit, knowing it's harmful and that we need to stop. Whenever I excelled at something, I felt guilty. I didn't feel I deserved it. I'd lower myself, then feel wrong because I knew I could do better. What leads you to feelings of guilt? When you see others less fortunate than yourself? When others envy you? Do you feel bad for not doing more to help another? Do you cheat on your spouse, steal, lie or keep secrets? Do you masturbate too much?

Where do these feelings come from? Where did we learn this behaviour? From our parents or teachers? Was it acquired from religion? Are the feelings of low self-worth legit or simply a projection?

Sin and virtue are two sides of the same coin. What's the difference between killing one man or one-hundred men? Does one make a war hero and the other a murderer? Who makes up these rules? I've learned all that matters is the intent behind the action. If something challenges my morals, I won't do it, and if it does, then I'll own it and let it go. We always do the best we can, and if we knew better, we would do better. Stop being so hard on yourself, and extend that to others. Whatever action is done cannot be undone, so what's the use of hanging on and replaying it? Let it go, or it will destroy you with depression and other destructive behaviour.

We must stop overcompensating with exaggerated attempts to please others. I tried making others happy by putting their needs before my own. I didn't want to make the wrong decision, or let anyone down. Lesson learned when an old man saw me struggling with a chain and lock. It was to rope off a rented parking spot behind the salon. Ice had shortened the chain and prevented me from securing it. I started to panic. I didn't want to get in trouble with the owner who was a nazi about keeping it secure. The man's words still echo in my mind, "Son, sometimes in life you just have to say... fuck it!"

## SHAME
*Guilt is the emotion you may feel after masturbating, shame is felt if you get caught.*

When an action we do relates to us, we feel shame, when it relates to another, it's guilt. This is another very destructive emotion responsible for destroying one's self-esteem, and is the core cause of depression, anger, addiction and suicide. I spent a good portion of my life feeling ashamed of who I was—loving myself was impossible. My capacity for intimacy, emotionally and physically was compromised, reduced by self-hate. I never felt good enough. I sabotaged my relationships before I got too close. I hid behind perfectionism and aloofness. When I wasn't hiding behind perfectionism and aloofness, I was drinking and acting like a clown. Both were responsible for my cherry coloured schnoz. "Rudolph the red-nosed reindeer—"

Adam and Eve is a symbolic story, and represents the male and female energies within us. The tale describes the innocence and naivety of a child living in paradise. When the serpent energy of the kundalini stirs during adolescence, it awakens the sexual urge. We are tempted to taste the fruit of knowledge— the pleasures of sexual exploration. The sacral chakra is the sexual centre of the body. It's also where guilt arises. Why do children not feel shame when naked? Why as adults do we feel the need to cover up?

## BLAME

When we blame a person or circumstance for our troubles, we are deflecting our responsibility for owning it. Denial makes everyone else accountable except for us. It's a lame alibi, projecting our crap onto others. When you point a finger at someone, you have three pointing back. Internal blame perpetuates the victim role, while projecting it toward another, spawns the bully. Continued self-blame can lead to guilt, shame and regret, and may also lead to depression.

Perhaps your parents betrayed you in some way, and you still hold it against them? Maybe it's their fault you turned out bitter and angry? Let it go. Stop making excuses. It took me a long time to take responsibility for my actions and behaviour. An abusive parent can cause their child to become compassionate or merciless, it depends on the interpretation. The same boiling water can soften the hard carrot, or harden the soft egg, which are you? I was both, until I learned to become tea and allow the harsh temperature to distil compassion from the dried leaves of my ignorance.

I directed a lot of blame toward my parents. I felt they should have known better, and parented me accordingly. Why did my father spoil the crap out of me and make me ill-prepared for the real world? Why wasn't my mom more open and able to talk, without assuming or closing off? Why did they check out when I needed them most? Why did my hockey coach play his son and his friends more than me? Why did my parents not learn and teach me English before school? Why did they stop speaking Italian when I did? Because they were doing the best they knew how. That was then and this is now. All is forgiven. It was that way for a reason—so I could learn my lessons.

What and who do you blame when your life sucks? Is it your family, your boss, the government, society's crumbling values, the youth of today, technology, the world going to shit? What about terrorists, your former or current spouse, lover, brother, sister, or in-laws? Did your child turn out different than you wanted? Are they gay? It could be that an uncle touched you where he wasn't supposed to. Were you betrayed by a person you trusted? Did they rape you? More on this shortly, as I will share a personal unpleasant experience with you. Would you accuse the dealer who gave you your first hit of heroin? Do you blame karma, your astrological sign, religion—God or Satan? You might blame the economy, stock market, rising food prices, gas and electricity? Maybe you blame yourself. Is it all your fault? What is stopping you from taking responsibility to change what needs to be changed now?

## COMPLAINING

Somehow we are under the impression that if we complain about something long enough, it will be resolved. How is that working for you? The more we whine about something, the worse it gets. The trouble is, this only pisses everyone off. If we're not part of the solution, we're part of the problem. I get it. Sometimes people suck, and we're compelled to let them know. No matter how much something pisses you off, the person or situation won't change if you're going to attack them. Are there people in your life that constantly bitch about something? Don't get sucked in—walk away.

## JUDGMENT

*"Stop trying to tell me what to do, cuz you don't even have a clue. Look into the mirror next time you do, now who is pointing at you?" Excerpt from the song 'Live My Life' 1987 by Frank Di Genova*

Viveka in Sanskrit means spiritual discrimination—right understanding. When we find fault, this triggers a conditioned reaction. When we're mindful we have clarity and compassion, there is no censuring. Every time we judge, it reveals an unhealed part in us, and is a form of inner resistance. Likewise, when a judgment against us causes a reaction, a raw nerve is in need of tending. Why do we put others down if they haven't threatened us? Would we need to? It seemed that every time I'd judge a person or a situation it would come back to me. I became what I judged. I'm convinced the universe does this on purpose—to teach us not to assume anything.

Separating and labelling is great for sorting out spices in our kitchen and chemicals in a lab. The moment we call something beautiful or ugly, it's isolated. It becomes comparable to something else. One isn't better than another. All is preference. Judgement is born of duality. It creates polarization. Are we taught to judge things as being good or bad? Or is it a natural response? Do we socially agree on what others have decided en masse? Or does it reflect our collective consciousness?

Over many years and throughout different cultures, the desired shape of a woman's body has changed many times. Plastic surgery has proven anatomical symmetry doesn't assure beauty—nothing is perfect. We must stop trying to force the puzzle piece into the wrong hole, as each one has its special place. We are unique, and all are needed to complete the grand puzzle. Doesn't it suck when there's one piece missing? The next time you step in shit, remember it's responsible for growing the beautiful flower.

A Chinese parable:

An old farmer was working in his field with his sick and aging horse. Feeling compassion for his horse, he set him free, and took him to the mountains to live out the rest of his life in peace. Neighbours from the nearby village heard the news, and offered their condolences. "What a shame your only horse is gone. How unfortunate. You must be sad. How will you live and work the land, and prosper?" The farmer replied, "We'll see."

A few weeks later, the old horse returned looking rejuvenated. The fresh mountain air and eating wild grasses had returned the horse to good health. It didn't take long for the villagers to come and congratulate the old farmer's good fortune. "You are so fortunate, you must be happy?" The farmer quietly said, "We'll see." At first light the next morning, the farmer's only son attempted to retrain the wild horse. He was thrown off and broke his hip. The villagers arrived and grieved over the farmer's latest misfortune. "What a tragedy. Your son won't be able to help you on the farm. How will you survive, you must be upset?" The old farmer didn't appear to be upset and simply answered, "We'll see."

Weeks later a war broke out. The Emperor sent his men to all the villages and demanded every young man fight with his army. The farmer's son was considered unfit to fight due to his injury. Again the villagers said, "You have good fortune!" as they watched their young sons march away. "You must be happy?" "We'll see," said the farmer, again. As time went on the farmer's son continued to suffer from his broken hip, and limped with pain. The farmer again was told how unfortunate he was. "You poor man, having to work alone until your son's hip heals." "We'll see," he said.

As it turned out, all the other young village boys died in the war. The old farmer and his son were the only men able to work the village fields. He and his son became wealthy, yet they were very generous to the villagers. "Oh, how fortunate we all are, you must be happy to share your good fortune?"... to which the old farmer replied, "We'll see!"

*The antidote for judgment is acceptance.*

## IMPATIENCE

I could write a book on impatience. Well, at least here is a section on it. I wasn't a patient boy, yet I've grown to be a patient man. I've learned expectation almost always leads to disappointment. I would sit in meditation for hours and think; hurry up inner peace, I don't have all day. My watch seemed to run slower than I wanted, the seconds never ticked fast enough. Now I wish they'd slow down. I have learned to trust and accept Divine time, and is probably why I don't wear a watch anymore. They say patience is a virtue, and all good things come to those who wait. How do we learn patience when we live in an instant gratifying world? God forbid, we don't get our burger before we drive up to the second window.

Christmas was always an exciting time for me. I loved it all: family, food and presents. I couldn't wait to open my gifts— literally. Christmas morning you'd find me alone by the tree, waiting for my parents and sister to get out of bed. It didn't concern me that it was only 6:00 a.m. Hurry up! Let's open the presents already. By the time everyone got up, dressed, and did their hair, (can't forget breakfast) I was going batshit crazy. Mom had to look good for the pictures. Dad had to set up his ancient Canon AE-1 camera, and on it went. I never understood why Mom even bothered. She never liked being photographed and avoided it whenever she could. What a production. This wouldn't do.

Being the resourceful little brat that I was, I devised a plan for the following year. Mom always put the presents under the tree a few days before Christmas. It wasn't her style to have a beautifully decorated tree without the picturesque boxes underneath.

"'Twas the night before Christmas, when all through the house, not a creature was stirring, except for this mouse. He took his dad's razor and snuck down to the tree, sliced open the paper for he wanted to see. He taped it back up so no-one would know, the little mouse knew, and put on a good show." I slit the tape, took a peek, and resealed the present. I can't believe they fell for it. Faking my surprise, though, wasn't fun. Not only did I fool them, I cheated myself.

## MISTRUST AND CONTROL

To live in society, we have to place our confidence in others to do the things we can't. This is difficult for most, especially for those who have issues with trust. We trust the bus will be on time, our waiter will get our order right, and our teacher will mark our test properly. Trust and control problems originate from the same source, a past trauma and the fear of it happening again. By trying to control an outcome, we attempt to micromanage situations, others and ourselves. When we do, we unconsciously project our hurt onto others, by bullying or manipulating them. Some may try to control an outcome by purging after they eat too much, or inflict self-harm to manage their emotional pain. The only way to trust another, is to trust yourself. Compassion gives others the safety to express themselves, without them feeling vulnerable.

I knew of a family that adopted an abused dog. It didn't trust people and nipped them. It took twelve years of constant love and patience for that dog to fully trust again. When it finally felt safe, it showed it was a loving dog. People are no different. We've all felt betrayed, abused and abandoned to some degree. We've all been affected by what we've buried deep inside, from childhood. Contrariwise, those who are too trusting set themselves up to be manipulated, and are easily taken advantage of.

## SUFFERING

*"Fear is the path to the dark side. Fear leads to anger. Anger leads to hate. Hate leads to suffering." Master Yoda*

How much do you believe your soul needs to suffer? There are two types of suffering, emotional and physical. There is a deep-seated belief in our DNA that we must suffer before anything good can happen to us. We learn this from witnessing our parents struggle, and from religion and society at large. I used to wear it like a badge, and made sure people knew. I suffered for the sake of suffering—it was my identity. When I was happy, or something good happened to me, I'd get worried it wouldn't last, or I'd have to pay for it later. Who was I to deserve it? That, to me, was selfish. I didn't feel good enough to receive love and abundance in my life.

We all have crosses to bear. The struggle strengthens us and is a great teacher. The problem is when we hold on to what's causing us the pain, we punish ourselves by not letting go. Hanging on to old belief systems, staying in an abusive relationship or the job that is slowly killing us, are just two examples. Why are we afraid to know who we are without struggling? Do we choose to suffer because we are afraid of change? The only thing that doesn't change is change, so why hang on? We either surrender to what is arising, or resist it. One way is easy and the other, painful.

It's a paradox, as suffering is needed in order to realize it's not needed. When we resist this very moment, we are not allowing it to be what it is. Our desire to change it, creates resistance, which in turn, creates the struggle.

## VAMPIRE

Although believed to be folklore, I am convinced there are vampires walking among us. Not in the traditional sense Hollywood portrays, but energetically, in the form of energy parasites. Our body requires food, water and oxygen to survive, but without *life force* none of these things can sustain it. If this were true then you could shove food into a dead person's body and revive it. Cosmic energy sustains all living things, and has many names. The Chinese call it *Chi*, the Japanese *Ki*, the Hindus call it *Prana* and the Egyptians refer to it as *Ka*.

This energy has varying polarities, with the higher and lower vibrations sensed as either love or fear. Like energies attract, and whichever is focused on, manifests our experience. When we are in ego, we perceive separation and feel cut-off from the collective, which triggers our survival mode. We become fearful, sense lack, and deplete our energy. What will a starving person do to satiate their hunger? Will they starve or steal to survive? Some have consciously and unconsciously learned to feed off other peoples energy.

A famous Cherokee Legend:

An old Cherokee is teaching his grandson about life. "A fight is going on inside me," he said to the boy. "It's a terrible fight and it's between two wolves. One is evil, and he is anger, envy, sorrow, regret, greed, arrogance, self-pity, guilt, resentment, inferiority, lies, false pride, superiority, and ego."

"The other is good and he is joy, peace, love, hope, serenity, humility, kindness, benevolence, empathy, generosity, truth, compassion, and faith. The same fight is going on inside you, and inside every other person too." The grandson thought about this, then asked, "Which wolf will win?"

The Grandfather simply replied, "The one you feed."

## DRAINERS

Have you ever met someone and suddenly felt weak or light-headed afterward, as if the life had been sucked right out of you? This can only happen if a part of you is vulnerable and resonates in like vibration with them. You let them in, through your compassion, sadness, insecurity, lack of self-worth, or need for approval. Energy vampires prey on a person's weakness, by literally plugging in to the person's energetic body. You can identify a drainer by how you feel around them. If something feels off, trust it. What often happens is we dismiss it or make excuses, but your intuition is never wrong. Sudden weakness, headaches, pain, and thoughts you don't normally have may be signs you've been plugged in to (corded). When we share a positive experience with another, we feel alive and empowered, not drained.

In my thirty years behind the chair, I've come across every type of energy drainer. The nature of my job puts me in a vulnerable position. Not only am I in close proximity to a client, but I touch part of their physical body. There would be days when I was literally wiped out. I had no idea how to properly protect myself, and absorbed all their fear. I am sensitive to energy, so I can tell immediately when someone isn't aligned to their highest self. There are physical things to look for if feeling energy isn't your thing.

People who: constantly whine and complain with no desire for a solution, are blamers and criticizers, who judge you, kill your creativity and stifle your ability to voice your thoughts, are close talkers, constant talkers, drama queens, poor me victims and people that try to intimidate you, never answer you directly and keep changing the subject when you ask them a direct question, give you the silent treatment, cutting you off mid-sentence, aloofness, and liars.

The next time you encounter a drainer, pretend you have diarrhoea and run to the bathroom... just kidding. It's a good idea to politely remove yourself and find your composure. Just don't engage in their shit. Raise your energy and stay positive.

Maybe you're the one who is energetically draining another. Do you feel empowered after hanging out with a friend? Are they yawning or laying on the ground unconscious afterwards? Codependent behaviour may be an indicator you're an energetic vampire.

Are you negative, play the victim, and complain about everything? Do you lie, act aloof, and always find you're late for things? Is manipulation something you resort to, for getting what you want? Do you prey on another's emotions using guilt, charm, flirting, or by force and intimidation? Are you a person that baits another by outrageous or violent behaviour, or by empty promises? Do you invoke jealousy or give a person the silent treatment? Do you put pressure on others or bring up old wounds to win an argument? If you do, then take a look at what you are trying to protect within yourself. We all have wounds in need of healing.

# CHAPTER FIVE

# SHATTERED ILLUSIONS

*"As the stark reality bursts through our innocence, the image in the mirror shatters into fragments. No longer do we try to see. Instead, we hide behind these fractured illusions and deny ourselves the love we are afraid to feel. We push away what we don't want to face. Or, cut ourselves with the shards of glass as we try to put ourselves back together." The Poem 'Shattered Illusions' 2016 by Frank Di Genova*

Which reality do you choose, the one that's happening now causing you pain, or the one where it didn't happen at all? Denial is a coping mechanism that buys us time, and is a way to deal with an uncomfortable experience. Withdrawing can lessen the severity of a trauma, as it enables us to enjoy life to the best of our ability. There is a reason why Cleopatra never went to a psychiatrist—she was The Queen of Denial.

## DENIAL

When a painful memory is held and buried, where does it go? Eventually it will surface, and when it does, it may be more than we bargained for. Denial isn't always about burying memories. It can be about making them up.

I was talking to a friend who recently lost her mother. She couldn't look me in the eyes. I said, "Hey I'm over here," while moving my index finger from her focal point to me. Her response was, "I can't. If I do, I will start to cry". She was drinking heavily and told me she was doing a lot of that lately. Denial may lead to addiction, and may also be the reason why it keeps us there. Everyone has their own way of deflecting attention from their pain, by acting aloof, blaming, or by being manipulative.

The more I accept my past and the more objective I am with it, the less it defines me. All my yesterdays are stories I acted in. There's no need to pretend they didn't happen. The account I'm going to share with you could have affected me in different ways. One was to deny it ever happened, and bury it deep in my subconscious. Two, I could have played the victim, and looped the experience in my head until it became my identity. Or three, I could have sought revenge and repeated the pattern, punishing whoever I thought deserved it. Fortunately, I didn't choose any of the above.

I was in grade five, and walking home from school with my best friend. We were cornered by a bunch of older boys who were in grade seven. They forced us into a nook of a townhouse complex where the residents put their garbage. No-one could see us. We were threatened with a knife and forced to drop our pants and do acts on each other. It was traumatic to say the least. What we decided to do afterward was courageous. It could have stayed a secret forever or we could tell the school principal what had happened. It was scary, we didn't know if anyone would believe us. What if the bullies got away with it and really hurt us for snitching on them? As fate would have it, the principal believed us, and all we had to do was pick them out of a line. They were expelled from school.

## PROJECTING

Projection is another form of denial. We defend ourself and don't admit to certain behaviour. We shift blame onto another so we don't have to acknowledge it. Our ego never wants to admit to being dysfunctional, so it pawns it off.

I was once on a dating site, and wrote my profile in a sexually suggestive way. It was a romantic dream sequence, nothing crude. Playful and sensual, my intention was to evoke passion. I received many responses, they ranged from disgust to admiration. One woman accused me of being a perverted porn writer, another a sicko, yet most of them were compliments. I was told by some that I *got it* and understood how to arouse women. A few even told me to write literotica. Then there was Jackie, she called me a male slut—how could I write something like this? I played along, and after a few emails, I must have gained her confidence. Out of the blue she started to tell me how she liked it, her favourite positions, along with her sexually dark fantasies. She wanted to meet right away and act out her forbidden desires. I didn't oblige.

One of my clients accused his wife of cheating on him. She wasn't, and as it turned out, he was cheating on her. He was diverting his unfaithfulness, so he wouldn't appear to be guilty. Then there was Andrew, he was almost fired from work because a very attractive woman accused him of making sexual advances in her office. He was upset and told me it wasn't true, she was hitting on him. Andrew later found out that she was attracted to him. She turned it around because of office policy regarding sexual harassment and relationships. It was her way of dealing with a potential problem.

Whenever you hear someone say, "That person's a cheap bastard," what they're really saying is, "I'm cheap, but not as much as they are. So, technically I'm not." The next time you feel a certain way about someone, take a moment and see if it's not you projecting onto them. They may be a mirror reflecting back facets of what you don't want to see in yourself.

## MIRROR

*I'm your reflection and you are me, I am your mirror when you fail to see. Every time you point your finger at me, it's you, you really see. If you want to be set free, start loving what you see." Excerpt from the song 'Reflection' 2013*
*by Frank Di Genova*

During my frequent visits to the local spiritual bookstore, I would occasionally see an author do a book signing. On one particular day I noticed a man sitting in a chair with a little table in front of him, his books stacked in a pile. The concept of a book signing was foreign to me at the time, so I didn't know what was going on. There was a long line of people waiting to meet him and have their book signed. My initial reaction was... *Who the hell was this guy? What an ego trip.* I was standing across the room when he caught me staring at him. It was like he sensed my thoughts. He grabbed my gaze and wouldn't let it go. I felt so uncomfortable. Really, he's staring me down? His eyes locked dead on mine, unflinching, powerful, yet gentle. I felt vulnerable and exposed. What was he doing to me? I had to leave.

A month or so later, I noticed a bestseller in hardcover format on the front shelf titled, The Power of Now, by Eckhart Tolle. It captivated my interest, and after reading a few pages I bought it. I looked at the bio and noticed the picture before I reached the cashier. That's when my mouthed dropped...

*No way. It can't be. But it was. It was the dude I'd seen at the book store.* Eckhart Tolle, was unknown at the time, at least to me. Everyone we meet is a mirror, reflecting back to us unhealed parts of ourselves that we often can't see on our own. Eckhart didn't project anything on to me, he was just observing. It was all my shit—my ego. Mr. Tolle if you ever read this book, I want to say thank you for showing me my pain body. If we ever meet again, may the stillness between us reflect back both love and gratitude.

Have you ever noticed when you meet someone for the first time, you either like them or not? Sometimes you're indifferent, with no reaction at all. Have you ever noticed we behave differently with each person we meet? These contrasts are due to the differences within us. I noticed this at my high school reunion. No matter how much time passes, some things don't change. It was strange, I noticed the same feelings of confidence and insecurity being triggered in me, by the same people, twenty-five years later. Mind you, the intensity of those feelings were less, compared to the level it was back then.

When we admire a behaviour in another, we're actually acknowledging and admiring that behaviour in ourself. The same goes for what irritates us, what we dislike and refuse to see in ourself is cast right back at us. In the next chapter I will discuss more on this regarding relationships. Sometimes it isn't a person that set us off.

## TRIGGERS

I must suffer from misophonia, a condition that drives people nuts when they hear certain sounds. It's ironic, as I am typing these words a dog is barking outside, distracting me. My neighbour next door has been pounding, drilling and sawing, seemingly forever. How long does a basement renovation take? People who suffer from this affliction may be dealing with anxiety and meet the criteria for obsessive-compulsive disorder (OCD). I'd prefer not to label myself with having anxiety or OCD. Though, I think we all have varying degrees of it. I'm tolerant of most sounds, but some, like a leaky faucet or people who pop their gum and chew it with their mouth open, drive me crazy. When I was a child and my father clipped his nails, I went insane. I still do when anyone does. When my mother ate crisp apples, it had the same affect. I always thought they did it on purpose, to upset me. What if misophonia was just a label, and there was something much deeper that affected our hatred of sound? What if it's not the barking dog, or the slurping of soup?

A trigger is something that sets off a reaction that's been anchored within the body/brain via the senses. It releases an intense memory, emotion, trauma, or injustice, to you or a loved one. The prompt is a mirror of something that has lain dormant until it's button has been pushed. Triggers aren't always negative. They can activate uncontrollable laughter and happiness. In NLP (Neuro Linguistic Programming) there is a technique called anchoring, where an internal response is anchored to an external or internal trigger. Russian physiologist Ivan Pavlov discovered if he rang a bell every time a dog ate, it would anchor a time to eat response. After a number of repeated procedures he could activate the same reaction by simply ringing the bell. Even without the food, the dog would salivate. Some triggers are knee jerk reactions, like when a doctor hits your knee with the little hammer.

Our subconscious mind induces these quick responses as a coping mechanism, to keep us safe when there could be potential danger. Unfortunately, some reactions aren't the most desirable, and can get us into trouble. We usually blame what triggers us and attack it, much like modern medicine treats the symptom and not the cause. When we understand why we're being set off, we can identify and release our unhealthy associations to it. When we no longer react, we are free.

I was cutting a new clients hair many years ago, and out of the blue she said to me, "I like you and want to continue liking you... but please stop touching me like that." I had no clue what she was talking about. I ran a mental movie of the previous ten minutes and couldn't figure out what it was. I was just touching her head. Then it hit me. Was it when I rested my hands on her shoulders to listen to her talk? The rest of the haircut was awkward. I did my best not to touch any part of her body, except for her hair. What had happened to make her react like that? My actions had definitely set something off and whatever it was, she mirrored something back at me to address. Was I too flirtatious? Had I touched her inappropriately? I couldn't blame it on being a passionate Italian man, could I?

Our physical senses can invoke memories: a familiar smell, a song on the radio, even a gentle caress on our body. They can bring us back to a fond memory, or an intense experience. Our parents are the best triggers, and are the masters and keepers of our launch codes. I knew a woman who would snap every time she was confronted. She could be waiting in a line up, and everything would be cool, until someone pissed her off. It could be anything: a look, the wrong tone of voice, whatever—she was a time bomb. Her way of dealing with this was to beat the crap out whoever pissed her off. Her mantra was do no harm, but take no shit. The trouble was she looked for it, and seemed to cause havoc wherever she went. That was her pattern.

## PATTERNS

*History doesn't repeat itself, patterns do.*

Patterns are ingrained reactions to situations that we keep repeating, usually, unconsciously. The way to break these behavioural algorithms, is to identify them so they can be released, before they get us in a serious rut. What patterns do you repeat? Do you attract the same type of emotionally unavailable partner/lover? Do you lose weight and then gain it back? Do you make friends and they stab you in the back? Do you attract the same situations in your life?

How do patterns form? Maybe as a little girl you witnessed your father leaving your mother, or as a boy, you saw your mom belittling your dad, and vice versa. Could these experiences create a sense of abandonment and low self-worth, that result in attracting unavailable and domineering partners later in life? I believe subconsciously we attract similar people and recreate the same situations, in an attempt to heal ourselves from these patterns. Next time you notice a pattern and question why it keeps occurring, consider what may have caused you to attract it in the first place.

My fear of rejection locked me in, 'I will not make the first move' paradigm. I would hang out with the girl I liked and hope she would make the first move, or at least show me she was interested. If she didn't, I assumed she wasn't into me. This spared me the humiliation of being rejected. What ever happened to the suave little boy who would go up to girls and kiss them on the lips? Something must have happened along the way that made me feel insecure, and warned me to protect myself. What was I afraid of? Was there an imaginary guillotine looming over my head?

When we identify a pattern, we are able to gain a higher perspective, and understand why we're on continuous replay. We peel off another layer of fear and ignorance. We keep attracting something until we pay attention to it, and when we do so, without resistance, it starts to dissolve. Are there any patterns you've overcome? What have they taught you? Each time we repeat a sequence, we meet it again. However, not at the same level. It's like walking up a spiral staircase, the experience feels more objective with each step and with less emotional investment. Maybe you believe a pattern is just another word for a habit?

## HABITS

When I first decided to have chocolate and cognac after dinner, it was a decision, but after the fiftieth time, it was no longer a choice but a habit. To me, patterns have more to do with early programming and how they affect us. Habits are acquired and play a different role. Learning guitar was hard for me at first. Now I play it without even thinking. Once my brain created more efficient ways to make playing it easier, it became second nature. I consider a good habit—when looking on the bright side of things—is brushing your teeth daily. Bad habits can be considered eating junk food, biting your nails, drinking and smoking. Repeating behaviours that give pleasure may also lead to addiction. Some say habits and addictions are one in the same. I think there's a difference. If stopping a behaviour we use to mask a discomfort is difficult, perhaps it's more than just a bad habit.

Repeated behaviour turns into a default setting, and causes us to operate on autopilot. This is beneficial, and helps us do tasks with less effort and more efficiency. Unfortunately, it's also a disadvantage. There were many times I drove to work and back, and couldn't remember driving the car. When I learned to drive manual for the first time, it was in rush-hour on a highway called The Don Valley Parkway, known as the Don Valley Parking lot. Traffic is stop and go on a good day, to say the least. I had to be mindful when switching gears, making sure I didn't stall the car, or ram it into the ass of the one ahead of me. I only stalled it twice. It didn't take long for me to stop remembering, and return to driving on autopilot.

As we become more efficient and less aware, being mindful is difficult. We can become lazy, careless, and stop thinking consciously. To offset this, we need to change things up, and do new things each day. Taking the path of least resistance is human nature, though, this keeps us in our comfort zone and can lead to procrastination. When a habit takes hold it's hard to break. We have to interrupt the action, and replace it with a better habit. When I quit smoking I took to eating pumpkin seeds, to satiate my residual hand to mouth habit. Thankfully, and to the delight of the drivers behind me, they no longer have to deal with flying shells hitting their windshield!

There are many schools of thought as to how many days it takes to create a new habit. It used to be twenty-one days, some say it's sixty-six, while others say it's eighty-four. I feel it can take longer, depending on your intent and reason. For example, I lost forty-one pounds in twelve weeks, by taking on a transformational body challenge. For three solid months I changed my eating and exercise habits, and the weight flew off. When the twelve weeks were over, I went right back to my old eating and drinking habits. Intent is the driving force behind everything. If it's not set properly, nothing will change. My intentions were set for all the wrong reasons. It may take years to make or break a habit or lifestyle, and can take one dramatic life experience to force you into it. Regardless, you have to really want to change. You can start by making small amendments until they become second nature.

## DISTRACTION

*The surest way to hell is trying to run away from it.*

Can you be alone with your thoughts? Does this freak you out? Do you get bored easily? Do you need sound from the tv or radio to keep you company? Are you constantly finding ways to stimulate your mind so you don't have to think about stressful things? Are you known for keeping busy by helping and caring for others, just so you can ignore your own problems?

We have lost touch with ourselves by the daily distractions we're bombarded with. Why can't we slow down? What are we afraid to face? Some memories are too painful to think about, let alone feel. Sometimes, the stress is too much to handle. When things do get excessive, we find ways to blow off steam and a good distraction is the best medicine. What if these ways of distraction become our vice instead?

I used to come home from a long day and go straight to the freezer. Waiting for me was my lover. She lay on her side, hibernating, covered in crystals. Every night I would rouse and empty her straight into a glass, then into my mouth. At times I would cheat on her, have an affair with her red and blonde friends. Sometimes all three of us played together. Beer was fun, she didn't hit me that hard. But those other two, especially if mixed together, were nasty. Vodka and wine, sure were crazy girls. Have you hung out with bad apples who pretended to be your friends, and who promised you the world? If so, who were yours?

Was it: the tub of ice cream, beer, wine, scotch... chocolate, anyone? Do you smoke it, eat it, drink it, snort it, or inject it? Am I being too harsh? Maybe you lead a healthier life. How often do you check your Facebook, email and texts? Have you downloaded candy-crush or farm-vile lately? Maybe you don't play video games, and aren't into technology, but do you watch tv, or binge watch any cool shows? What about unrestrained eating, shopping, gossiping, or sleeping all day? Overindulgence of sex, porn and masturbating also counts. What if all this isn't your style, and you're into health and fitness? Do you need to run twenty kilometres a day to get your runners high? Or do you freak out if you miss a workout? Are you orthorexic and need to consume only the healthiest of foods? Does your fat quota have to be under ten percent? Do you binge eat and purge?

I'm guilty with a lot of the aforementioned, so I'm not pointing fingers. We can get distracted with anything. No one is immune, and the more layers we uncover the more subtle they can be. I used to meditate too much, read too many books, and jump from one teaching to another. It doesn't matter if we're popping pills, obsessively calling our shrink, or over achieving—it's all the same. Simply put, we are avoiding pain.

## ADDICTION

*"Fighting a losing battle, with no intention to win, destruction to your body, every time the needle goes in. Melting your brain to jelly, with things that get you high, you're headed for the gutter, don't you know your gonna die?" Excerpt from the song 'You're Gonna Lose' 1988 by Frank Di Genova*

Whenever we hear about addiction, we automatically assume it's due to weakness or having no willpower. In most cases this isn't true. Experiencing any kind of trauma early in childhood may be responsible for the wounds we currently carry and try to protect ourself from. Since it's human nature to move towards a pleasurable experience, and away from a painful one, we shouldn't fault ourselves. We can be influenced by either. It depends on which is the stronger motivator, the consequence or the reward. In doing so, our instincts propel us toward the path of least resistance. Corporations, drug dealers, and the fast food industry are well aware of this. We are easy targets. Like shooting fish in a barrel, only the fish are jumping in on their own volition. The drive-thru has to be the greatest innovation so far, as you don't even have to get out of your car! This book could be about *how to get rich quick*. All you'd need to do is invent something that gives people the most amount of pleasure with the least amount of effort.

We all want to feel loved, accepted and have a sense of purpose. There is new research linking addiction to loneliness. This is not to be confused with being alone. The lack of connection, touch and being loved, can force one to look for it in other ways. Instead of having healthy relationships with others, we have them with our painkillers.

Addiction happens when large amounts of dopamine hijack our pleasure centre, and turn us into slaves. Normally, natural releases of dopamine brought on by moderate exercise, sleep and feeling love, are perfectly handled by our brain. When an unnatural level of dopamine is released, emotional ups and downs occur. When something like sugar or cocaine seizes the brain's pleasure centre, upward of ten times the normal amount of dopamine suddenly gets released into our system. The intense rush of ecstasy floods our body and eventually overloads our receptors and neurotransmitters. Our brain adapts and releases less dopamine, and increases our tolerance. This results in needing more stimulants, which further desensitizes our receptors giving us less and less pleasure. When we crash, it isn't pretty, and causes us to want more. This process taps out our adrenals, and exhausts our system. There is only so much abuse our body can take.

It takes a minimum of three days for our body to physically withdraw from stimulants, be it caffeine, sugar, or any type of drug (longer with benzodiazepines). Recalibrating and sensitizing our receptors takes longer—more so to fully remove the toxins from our systems. Unfortunately, it doesn't stop there. The emotional slavery can linger for weeks, months and even years later. As a result, we need to disrupt and change the neurological pathways that have formed. When I stopped smoking my craving was still there, even though the nicotine had left my system. It was the same when I quit drinking. My body didn't like it anymore. But I did because I was still emotionally enslaved to it. I could stop drinking alcohol and eating sugar for a day or two, no problem. I did so, many times, even for weeks at a time. The longer I stopped, my mind started to think, "*Man this shit's getting real. Do I really have to make a choice? Do I bite the bullet or say screw this and go back to my comfort level?*" Before we know it our excuses win out and we're off the wagon.

Alcohol and stimulants aren't the only way we can alter and desensitize our brain, we can be clean, drug free and still fall into addiction. Behaviour can affect our brain's chemistry, just the same. I was having sex with a former girlfriend in a woman's bathroom of a Japanese market. We got caught by an old woman. When she saw us doing the act over the sink, she screeched at the top of her lungs. The rush I felt having sex in public and feeling the risk of getting caught was exhilarating. Getting caught made me feel alive! It doesn't matter if it's video games, porn, extreme sports, gambling, high-stakes finance or having sex in public, it's a rush all the same.

When something beyond our conscious control happens to us, such as a traumatic life-changing experience, it can really fuck us up. A brain that's been to war is not the same as one that hasn't. First responders, emergency hospital staff, rape and abuse victims can all suffer from post-traumatic stress disorder (PTSD). In fact, it can happen to any of us at any time. In chapter eleven I share a technique that helps release traumatic experiences.

# CHAPTER SIX

# RELATIONSHIPS

*"Can't you see the reasons, why we can't go on? Like the change of seasons, fighting on and on." Excerpt from the song 'Can't You See?' 1985 by Frank Di Genova*

A relationship is an ultimate mirror. It exposes everything we hide from ourselves and brings out the best and/or worst in each other. It forces us to trust another with our emotions, and reveals our vulnerabilities. As a result, when a person enters a relationship they risk getting hurt, and feeling abandoned. Some avoid intimacy altogether. Susceptibility is not always the reason we avoid an emotional bond. It could be we don't want to give up the things we love, or we fear losing a sense of who we are. It may mean having to change into something we're not. Whatever the case, relationships force us to look past who we think we are.

I used to be the clingy type and often smother my partners. Now, this type of behaviour in a woman is what drives me away from her. Was it because I wasn't able to connect with my mother at birth that I wanted them to stay close? Regardless, I learned that neediness shows weakness, so I stopped being sticky.

There are two dominant fears in any relationship, abandonment and smothering. The one who fears abandonment is usually the one that clings. This creates a self-fulfilling prophecy that drives the other away. What we're initially attracted to in a partner typically ends up being the very thing that propels us to the door. As a teenager I was wild and out of control, like a mustang needing discipline. This was a cover for my pain. My former-wife was a no bullshit, straight to the point woman. At the time I needed that. Just a few years later, those very same traits drove me away.

Not all relationships are about lovers and spouses. There are different types, all with varying levels of mental, emotional and physical intimacy. There are bonds between parents, siblings, children, cousins, family, friends, teachers, coaches, coworkers, employers and so forth. Each one mirrors back different aspects of ourselves. These characteristics aren't typically seen on our own. Unconsciously, we look to another to define us, to complete us, and to make us feel happy. Unfortunately, this always ends in failure. No one is responsible for our happiness except for ourselves. If that sounds kind of harsh and self-centred consider this... Isn't it more selfish to impose that responsibility on another?

From an early age we rely on our parents to instil in us feelings of love and acceptance. Many don't experience this because their parents didn't either. This rings true for older generations who weren't taught how to express love in an open way. We are fortunate to live at a time where we're able to talk about our feelings openly.

My mother was one of seven children who worked on a farm. Her parents were simple and hard working people. In those days they didn't have family discussions. God forbid if one talked about their feelings. The stance was, "I'm the parent, follow the rules. Do what I say." Parents showed their love in different ways, by providing for and protecting their family. Even today, for some men, this is the only way they know how to express their affection. My father was never the touchy-feely type. He finds it uncomfortable to share his feelings freely. It's the same with my son. I guess I'm different. How else would I be able to write about this stuff?

## ADULTS VS CHILDREN

I can't count the number of times I've seen couples fight in public. Whether in the grocery store, out in the street, or when visiting friends, it happens everywhere. Aren't they aware that others are watching? Could they be doing it on purpose? Sometimes I think it is. Maybe they want someone to side with them, or they simply want the attention.

Not long ago I was at the grocery store shopping. I saw a young couple fighting in the same aisle ahead of me. Both took turns to yell and criticize the other. "You never listen to me," she said. "Ya, well you're a stupid complaining bitch," he countered, and on it went. When they weren't hollering they were giving each other the silent treatment. They blamed each other without even trying to understand what the other was saying. They acted like two kids fighting over a toy in a sandbox. I often wonder why people stay with a person they accuse of being stupid. What does that say about themselves?

In a healthy relationship, emotional maturity is imperative. So is mutual respect for one another. Quite a few years ago I was cutting a clients hair. We were discussing relationships. She said that her husband always wanted to have sex and complained that she never put out. She admitted doing it on purpose. I asked her why. She responded by saying, "The moment he stops treating me like his mother, he will get laid." It made perfect sense. This was an aha moment for me.

Women are not our mothers—men are not our fathers. Yet it seems that way in the relationships I've encountered. Two adults need to be present for a healthy relationship to thrive. There can not be a child and an adult in the dynamic—or in the story above, two children. Emotionally mature adults address and resolve conflicts as they arise. Children on the other hand only know how to kick and scream until they get what they want.

A few years back I had a woman friend at my place. We were kind of seeing each other, it was casual. We were in bed. She started complaining about something irrelevant. I can't even remember what about. All I know was, it was 2:00 a.m. and I just wanted to sleep. She kept fussing and didn't stop. I'd had enough. Finally with a stern voice I said, "If you want to act like a spoiled six year old brat, then get out of my bed now! It's time for you to go home! Come back when you grow up!" She picked up her clothes and started to dress. I was waiting by the door to escort her out. When she realized that I wasn't kidding, she undressed and slid back into bed. She placed her head on my chest and snuggled close not saying another word. That didn't sit well with me. I couldn't be with a girl. I wanted a woman.

## MY EXPERIENCE

I grew up believing that to be happy I had to get married, buy a house and have a family. At the time, my beliefs convinced me that I could find happiness through another person. This was true in the beginning, but only lasted for a short time. I had someone that understood me and gave me the emotional support I needed. It was us against the world. I thought being married and having children would be the panacea for all my problems. The concept is great. It's a good fairytale until real life plays out and the challenges appear. Don't get me wrong, I have great memories, and was in love with my wife at the time. I am grateful for my son and have no regrets for my ten years of marriage. They weren't all happy, and even less so during the end. Still, I wouldn't change a thing.

Life isn't a fairytale, it is a teacher. We learn by experience, not by what we are told. After my marriage failed, I thought the next relationship might be better. When that didn't work, I thought the next woman might be the one. I was running out of excuses, and people to blame. I soon realized that my unhappiness wasn't because I was with the wrong partner. The only person responsible for my failed relationships, was the man in the mirror looking back at me. After every failed relationship, came more despair. Each drove me deeper into self-doubt and depression. I was broken. I stopped believing that there was such a thing as a life partner or soulmate. The possibility of meeting *The One* was bullshit. Disney, Hallmark and Cupid were selling lies!

We all have patterns. Mine was to attract a woman who needed to be saved. Frank was the guy to mend their broken wings. He thought it was his job to free them of their pain. If I fixed them, certainly I would be worthy of being loved. My presumption was that they would see how much more I cared for them, than I did for myself. I thought, *look I'm putting you before me, isn't that the ultimate display of unconditional love?* It shocked me every time the relationship failed. After all my effort and dedication I'm still not good enough? "Fuck you, fuck all of you." I resolved to stay single. I'd rather be alone, than wishing that I was. I always gave too much, and got nothing back. *Why waste myself on someone who didn't appreciate me?* The problem was, I didn't appreciate me. What woman would want an insecure guy? Especially one that believed that they didn't deserve his love and dedication. How fucked is that?

Sex is always better when you have a real connection with someone. I wanted it to be mind-blowing. How could I have stupefying sex when I couldn't be vulnerable or trust the woman? I disliked being alone, but also disliked being in a shallow relationship. The conflict was killing me. I didn't want to become like some of my serial dating friends. They jumped from one relationship to another because they were afraid of being alone. I didn't want to settle or waste my time exploring. Why invest in someone that I felt wasn't capable of giving me what I wanted?

I was a magnet for married women. Not just one or two, but many. It was unreal. What happened to my ability to attract single women? Maybe I didn't want a real relationship and just pretended I did? Perhaps that power was safer turned off? Nonetheless, I loved the attention. I didn't sleep with any of them, but just knowing I could was enough. It was driving me crazy, I could have them but couldn't. What the hell was I doing? Who did I think I was? Casanova? I wanted to get out of this pattern, but how?

When I did meet a woman, I'd fall in love fast—head over heels. We'd always be together, kissing, touching and hugging. I could never get enough. I'd want to have sex all the time. I'd become so infatuated that I wouldn't notice any of her flaws or red flags. In fact, she made me forget my own. My mission was to captivate her, and to make love to her better than anyone else did. I wanted to be her God—serve and dominate her—save her from everything evil. I wanted her to become an insatiable sexual savage, unrelenting and yearning only for me. The more I got to know her, the more things I started to dislike. Was this woman someone I wanted to be with forever? As the pixie dust wore off, the arguments increased. I'd start to dismantle and reject every part of her. She wasn't the one. She never was.

I was called too picky, gay, and that I had unrealistic expectations. Was it all the porn and playboy magazines that had distorted my reality? Was I waiting for my magical unicorn? Why did I sabotage every single relationship? Was it because I was burned in the past? Were my expectations too high? She had to be beautiful, fun, smart, spiritual, non-materialistic and great in bed, but not a slut. My list was long. Women didn't have a chance. I set it up to make them fail. It was for my protection. No one was ever going to have the chance to reject me again. Not before I could. How could anyone love me if I couldn't? Would I ever be able to love myself unconditionally? The answer is, I have!

How about you? What do you desire in a partner? Are your expectations realistic? Can you be authentic with yourself? Are you carrying around any destructive emotions like guilt, anger, fear and shame? Are you bringing them into your relationships? Are you aware of your patterns? Are you attracting the same type of people—different but the same? Are they emotionally unavailable? Are they promiscuous, submissive, aggressive or controlling? What are you looking for? Is it the one? Or is it always the next one?

## EXPECTATION

What do you expect from a relationship, or partner? That question may vary depending on our gender, and what was imprinted on us by our parents. Our roles have changed and are not the same as our parents. These roles will change for our children, and for theirs. My father was the only son of my grandparents. He was the sixth sibling of their blended family. His mother was a widow. She had a son—his father was a widower who had four children. My grandmother needed a husband, as my grandfather did a wife. That's how it was back then, marriage was for survival as well as companionship. For many, it's still like this today. My reason for getting married was to provide me with a sense of completion, stability, and sex on demand. I needed to know someone loved me, no matter what. Does a piece of paper really have that much power?

If what you desire is the nice house, the white picket fence, kids, and a dog, then marriage is great. Having a family and watching your child grow is one of the best gigs out there. I am looking forward to meeting my grandchildren—God permitting. I wanted marriage more than anything. On a deep level, I still do, regardless of my past experience. Wedlock represents a mutual commitment between two people. Marriage is about co-creating and sharing. It brings everything to the table, the sunshine and the rain. More so when you have kids. When the husband becomes a father and the wife a mother, the relationship usually gets put on the back-burner. If an effort isn't made to keep the focus on the partnership—once the children have left the nest—you may feel as though you're living with a stranger.

Money and stress are the biggest challenges to any couple. So is fidelity, or the lack thereof. Sometimes a partnership comes to an impasse, and hard decisions have to be made. Do you stay for the sake of the children, the money, or the house? Do you fear being alone and that no one will want you? Is it better to have what you have now than nothing at all? Would you feel like a failure? There is a lot of conditioning that is still ingrained within us about marriage/relationships. It may be what's holding us in fear, and locked into patterns of feeling stuck.

Times are changing, and so are our needs. We no longer need a spouse in the traditional sense. Women are becoming more financially independent. Men are learning to cook, and clean the skid marks from their underwear. As more of our needs are met, we have an increased opportunity for self-exploration. This isn't always a good thing when it comes to a committed relationship. Sometimes couples don't always grow together. This can strain their connection. It is a gift when both can grow together equally, side by side. Personally I've learned that no one person can give you everything. This was a rude awakening for me.

It may take more than one relationship to find out what we truly want. As our awareness expands, different people are drawn to us. The potential for growth is available. This doesn't mean we need to audition a merry-go-round of partners. Emotions are at play and are delicate. If you change them like you do your underwear, people will get hurt. Where does it all stop? It takes at least four seasons to even begin to know someone. I feel it takes much longer. Some go on impulse, and jump straight into a committed relationship—declaring that they've found the one. Could it be from the high they feel from the love chemicals that are pumping throughout their body? I did it twice and almost three times. It only cost me two homes, and depleted me mentally and emotionally.

We usually want something we don't have. The challenge of the chase may be what motivates us. I can say from experience, the grass isn't greener on the other side. You may have a different address, but the problems will be the same. I've learned we take our garbage with us. We throw it at our new partner and see what sticks. *Here, take my trash and make it go away.* When they can't, we blame them for it.

When the high is gone and the orgasm is over we are left with the person. The one we've emotionally invested in. The one who didn't clean up our mess. Do you still love them? Have you become friends? Or has your bond been built only on sex—now boring and predictable? Do you take your circus on the road and look for another buyer? Or do you finally unchain your white elephants and free your mental monkeys?

## MY ADVICE

Decide on what you want in a relationship. There is no right or wrong. Be up front with your intentions. They should be transparent and mutually agreed upon. Respect each others boundaries. A solid relationship cannot be built on deceit. It boggles my mind how much more I know about my female clients than their own husbands/partners do. Let's face it, when it comes to playing games, both of our species have been known to use manipulation to get what they want.

The honeymoon stage keeps us on our best behaviour. However, when it's over we turn into pumpkins. We get too comfortable. Some guys turn into slobs. They fart, burp and their clothes somehow start missing the hamper and end up on the floor. When the clock strikes twelve, some gals become less adaptable. Their true motives surface and they start trying to change their man. Can we sue for false advertising? What happened to being authentic right from the beginning? It is better to be authentic than it is to hide. Everything eventually rises to the surface, so there is no use in camouflaging who we are. If you like masquerade parties you can always go to Italy. The Venice Carnival happens annually in February.

## WHAT IS THE PERFECT RELATIONSHIP?

There is no such thing as the perfect relationship or marriage. This is a flawed assumption. Why? Because it's based on an outward pursuit. The perfect relationship starts with you. Love yourself the way you want to be loved. Respect yourself the way you want to be respected. You have to know your own worth. You have to know and establish your boundaries. Make time for you, get to know yourself. Having the perfect partner has nothing to do with the other person. When we own our happiness we stop saying things like, "If you really loved me you would change." Your reality is yours, and their reality is their own. We are merely guests in each other's actualities. No one has the right to impose on the other. Be the person you're looking for. Then you'll have the perfect relationship.

When we learn how to communicate what we're feeling without blaming, our partner won't consider it an attack. They won't feel the need to defend themselves. It goes both ways. Couples will fight, it's part of the deal. Blackmail isn't. We are responsible for our actions, our feelings and emotions. Instead of focusing on what's wrong with our partner or relationship, focus on what's right. Align to what feels good, and to what expands your connection with them. Complaining only reinforces the problem, and doesn't offer a solution. Fretting grants the person an excuse to stray—to cheat. Guys, stand up and be a man, don't be an asshole. Take care of her, and be proud to walk alongside her. Gals, get in touch with your feminine power. You are not a victim.

Hollywood likes to blend couples names together to make one entity. A relationship is not about merging together. It is not about needing to change the other, or to make the other happy. This only creates resentment and means you'll lose yourself in the process. Kahlil Gibran wonderfully said, "Fill each other's cup but drink not from one cup. The pillars of the temple stand apart." My version is simple, "Share the toothpaste, not the toothbrush."

Trust, communication and respect are essential in any true relationship. It begins with you. Respect yourself and trust your intuition. Be clear with your intentions and communicate your needs. This applies to you, and your partner—mutual support.

You are good enough, and it's time to stop being so hard on yourself. You deserve the best. That means you do not settle for anything less than that.

## AWAKENING THE GOD AND GODDESS WITHIN

My mother and father were both born in Italy. They met and married in Toronto Canada. They had me two years later. I'm a hybrid of both Italian and North American culture—each have their own unique qualities. Learning to integrate the disparity between the two wasn't fun. Today, however, I'm grateful to have been given that chance. It has allowed me to gain a deeper perspective. In Italy, it's common for men to show their softer side. They carry a man purse, and keep up with the latest fashion. Although I'd argue with their choice of speedos at the beach. Italian men are passionate, love to cook and are close to their mothers (I wasn't until her last days). I remember my father telling me that he and his friends would walk down the street arm in arm. They were all attracted to women and saw nothing wrong with displaying brotherly love. I was shocked. I would never have attempted to do that here, not in this country.

In North American society, men are taught to be tough. Showing emotion is considered a weakness. In the past, movie idols like James Dean, John Wayne and Clint Eastwood were the male role models. They depicted masculinity. Rock Hudson was another, yet it wasn't until later that he came out and declared he was gay. Modern heroes such as Rambo and Conan the Barbarian embodied machoism—might is right. I didn't resonate with either the Neanderthal, or the overly sensitive guy archetypes. Where did I fit in? I wasn't gay or macho. Who could I emulate? Aside from spiderman and superman, my father was my role model. He wasn't the gushy emotional type. Men of that generation didn't openly show their emotions beyond anger and happiness.

Emotionally, I was a deep sea diver and had to settle for being a snorkeler. I had to fit in—it was eating away at me. I had no one to dive with. Sure, others were sympathetic and could understand. Empathy, however, is something different. Why were so many people closed off emotionally, choosing only to stay on the surface? Women were easier to hang out with than guys were. They understood emotions better. Yet, I could only handle them for so long. When my estrogen levels rose too high, I lost my bearing. It was the same in the dressing room, with the guys. It was the same banter—a broken record. How many chicks can I bang? How much weight can I lift? Who can drink more? Who's dick is bigger? There was only so much estrogen and testosterone I could handle at one time. Where was the balance between eat love pray, and eat fuck kill? Maybe I was just a freak of nature and didn't belong? Couldn't men and women embody both? Not in a bi-sexual way, but more balanced and less extreme. Was I on the leading edge—was I an evolving male? Whatever I was, I hid it well. It wasn't easy.

From what I've seen, it's more acceptable for a woman to express spirituality than a guy. Thankfully this is changing. I'm not the only guy attending spiritual workshops anymore. There are more males doing yoga and meditating. Last year a shaman led a group of women and myself in a sound healing ceremony. When it was over everyone shared their experiences. During the conversation the shaman said to me, "You know, it's harder for a man to show that he's spiritual than it is for a woman." I agreed and thanked him. He's the only person who has confirmed what I have been feeling for most of my life. Some of the women in our group didn't agree.

Writing this book is like *coming out* for me. I am exposing who I really am to my family and friends—to the world. They've all known I'm a bit different, yet now they will for sure. I can sympathize with people in the LGBT (lesbian, gay, bisexual, and transgender) community. Was my spiritual coming out less emotionally painful? I hid my spiritual side for the longest time, only revealing it when I was with like minded-people. This was especially true when dating. I quickly learned that talking spirituality didn't build sexual tension. "Hi, my name is Frank, I am a Reiki master. I can sense energy and feel your emotions. Do you want to shag?" It was straight to the friends zone. The best I got was a long hug. Eventually, I stopped hiding it and learned how to balance both aspects of myself. There is a time and place to talk about spiritual stuff.

Men tend to be more left brain dominant. This is associated with performing tasks, analyzing, and fixing things. Women are generally more right brain dominant. This corresponds with intuition, creativity, imagination and feeling. Beyond our physical attraction and the need to propagate our species, I believe there's a deeper reason why we're attracted to each other. We are evolving, not only mentally and physically, but spiritually as well. Inherent and equally within us, are both the masculine and feminine aspects. Spirit in its purest and non-physical form is neither. We experience this duality in the physical form.

The moment we're born, we take on the attributes of our gender. In time, we become fully identified with it. Perhaps this is why we crave our other half. To merge with our opposite gender—for a sense of completion. Man evokes the reasoning in the woman. Woman evokes the emotion in the man. We are striving for this balance within ourselves.

The Divine Feminine and the Divine Masculine is awakening. Women are becoming more independent—men are learning how to trust their emotions. Our roles are changing. There is progress in regard to this model, although there is still far to go. There remains resistance and confusion from both sides. This is normal when new paradigms emerge. In the past, patriarchy was required to build our society (world) as it has. Now, it's responsible for destroying it. War, government and extreme religion are corroding what it once built. The Goddess energy is awakening and is needed for the next step in our evolution.

We may not be burning women at the stake anymore, but there's still inequality. Men continue to dominate and suppress strong women. You can tell how evolved a culture/society is by how they treat their females. Lower conscious men fail to realize that all human life comes from a woman. At times, the pendulum swings too far one way, and this creates extremism. Unfortunately, until balance is achieved, there will be unconscious behaviour from both the male and female psyche.

Our evolution regarding relationships goes beyond that of emotional maturity. It begs for us to understand that it's a bond between two awakening souls. A conscious male and a conscious female.

## THE CONSCIOUS MALE

Walks his truth, without exception and is not afraid to take risks. If he makes a mistake, he owns it without needing to apologize, blame or criticize. He doesn't seek approval or need validation because he's in alignment with his purpose. He isn't wishy-washy and doesn't retreat when he is challenged (this allows a woman to trust him.) He can express his emotions without being emotional. He doesn't lose his temper, is compassionate yet strong. He is highly sexual, yet knows how to seduce and build sexual tension without objectifying a woman. He can make her feel safe and comfortable so she can explore her sexuality without the fear of being judged. He doesn't categorize and judge all women to be the same, regardless of his past experiences. He knows how to challenge them, and empowers them to be the best they can be. He loves himself (not conceited) and it shows, people want to be around him.

## THE CONSCIOUS FEMALE

Has embraced her feminine power. Wants a man yet doesn't need him. Doesn't see herself as a victim. Can be open while hurting physically and emotionally. She can express and communicate her needs clearly. Has emotional strength and maturity. Is patient, trustworthy and has compassion. Has integrity and doesn't settle for anything less than she is worth. Respects herself in every way. She expects a man to engage her beyond her body. She wants him captivated by her emotional depth, intelligence and creativity. Loves men, and allows them to be masculine. Her desire is to nurture, not to fix his wounds. She sees his potential, supports and inspires him. Her desire is more than the material things. She loves herself, embraces her beauty and sees it in all things. She can receive openly. Is not in competition with other women and fully supports them. She is courageous when faced with the unknown.

Ultimately, we seek our own evolved self in each other. When we honour these characteristics within ourself first, we can then behold them in our beloved.

## COMMON RELATIONSHIPS

*Men: "Give a woman an inch and she'll take a mile."*
*Women: "Ask a man for an inch and he'll give you a mile."*

I believe we have distorted expectations about marriage/ relationships learned as children. Unrealistic stories read to us about the prince saving the princess then living happily ever after. As a little girl were you planning your wedding day at the tender age of three? Were you taught as a boy to be strong, and real men don't cry? Was there a disconnect from mom and dad's relationship in comparison to what you saw in fairytales?

Do we put the onus on our lover to make us happy? The next time we demand change from our partner, consider how hard it is to change even a small behaviour in ourself. Nobody is flawless. Trying to change your partner to conform to your needs only pushes them away. It creates resentment, as well as being unfair.

Success in any relationship requires us to allow the other their authenticity. It means allowing them the confidence to be able show up, fully, with no masks or modifications. They are your mirror, if you are not happy, it's not their fault. We are not responsible for saving anyone. People change because they want to, not because we need them to.

I am not suggesting we bail at the first sign of a disagreement. It takes effort, desire, and honest communication to keep it going. We either give up too easily, or stay in the same toxic relationship because of financial reasons, tradition, or for the sake of the children. If it's because of the children, they can sense when their parents are unhappy. For a relationship to be successful it takes two to be onboard. If one isn't, then nothing will make it work.

Love, honour and respect yourself. Know your boundaries, and align to what you deeply desire. Only then will you be a match to someone who wants the same. The deeper you can love and accept yourself, is the depth to which you will be able to love another.

# CHAPTER SEVEN

# HOLOGRAPHIC UNIVERSE

*"Close your eyes and drift away, to a world that's okay... and before you know the night becomes the day... and your senses start slipping away." Excerpt from the song 'Dreaming' 1986 by Frank Di Genova*

What if we were living in a holographic universe? In a world created by varying levels of condensed energy? What if this book that you're holding isn't as real as you think?

Imagine if all that we see in this dimension is just an illusion. No, I'm not having an acid flashback... those days are long gone. Most of us know about 3D technology—it brings to life a flat two-dimensional image into realistic imageries. It is similar to how our human eyes perceive objects. As a child, I would often dream of playing a video game where I could walk and play as if it was a real world. The floor would be a moving conveyer belt within a dome structure. Lasers would project three-dimensional images of dragons that I'd kill with my special sword. When the blade would touch the beam, the enemy would perish. Wouldn't that be cool? Could it be that the technology has existed for eons of time?

In Hindu philosophy, it is considered that we exist in an illusionary world, where a Divine dream play was created by an infinite supreme consciousness, many call God. This concept suggests that reality is just a mirage that deludes us. Maya is the Sanskrit word for illusion, and is responsible for creating this deception. There may be more to this world than meets the eye. We may exist in a reality composed of energetic grids that are created on patterns of sacred geometric blueprints. Could our body, it's DNA, snowflakes, flowers, petals, and basically everything in the physical form, emerge from these energetic grids?

I'm a fan of certain genres of science fiction. Notably the ones that intelligently ask, "What if?" What were movies like 'The Matrix', 'Inception', and 'The Thirteenth Floor' implying? Technology seen in the 'holo-deck' in Star Trek, and the 'halo-band' in the short-lived Caprica series, explored these future possibilities. Perhaps they suggested that we may be under their spell right now. Have you ever had a dream so vivid that you swore it was real—until you woke up? Or, are you still sleeping?

Assuming we do exist in a simulated reality, could it be manipulated by focusing our willpower on it? What if we are affecting it and don't realize we are? Do you believe life happens to you? Or is it your belief you make it happen? If you knew that you were the writer, producer, director and actor of your life, would you change it? How would you live then, knowing that you were the judge, the jury and the executioner of your thoughts, feelings and actions?

What if everything you thought that was happening outside of you, was really happening within you? If this world isn't real and it's an illusion, or a game, could it be that we are actors in the play as well as the audience? Could we be the observer that is witnessing the performance?

## DIMENSIONS OF REALITY

The *Zero dimension* is the holder, the space in which all things are created—the black hole. At its centre is what physicists call the "singularity", the point where extremely large amounts of matter are squeezed into an infinitely small amount of space. There are no measurable aspects. Yet it's one of the most powerful things in the universe.

The *First dimension* is measurable, such as the length of a line. When you connect the two end points you get a one dimensional object.

The *Second dimension* is measurable in two ways, length and width. It's a flat world, like a shape that's drawn on a piece of paper, such as a triangle, square or circle and so forth.

The *Third dimension* is the physical world (physical awareness.) Time and space is the container in which this hologram is projected. Our concept of time is in linear measurement, and occurs in sequence—before, during and after. There are six directions: up/down, left/right, and front/back. Other movements are variations of these basic directions. It's interesting to note that there is no in/out. This applies to our awareness of moving through each plane. The physical world is polarized and perceived in duality: hot/cold, hard/soft, and good/bad and so on. Our physical senses are limited to and perceived by, only that which is resonating in the *Third dimension*. What if there exists other electromagnetic frequencies that vibrate beyond the known nine kilohertz to three thousand gigahertz range? Who's to say there aren't other frequencies oscillating beyond the known electric and radio waves, such as: infa-red, ultra violet light, X, gamma, and cosmic rays.

The *Fourth* and *Fifth dimensions* exceed the scope of our five senses, yet psychics and empaths are able to tune in, and communicate on other spectrums of vibration. They are more sensitive than those that are not willing to accept a reality beyond what they see, touch, hear, smell, and taste. I believe fear and our identification to our body is what keeps us bound to this dimension. It numbs our sensitivity to the ethereal dimensions.

The *Fourth dimension* (soul awareness) is the astral plane (astral world). Shamans call it the spirit world, and the Egyptians refer to it as the Duat. Every culture has their own name for it. This realm resonates behind the veil of our third-dimensional world. It exists in non-time, and is non-physical. Past, present and future timelines coexist simultaneously. This is the place where our dreams occur. When we dream, our astral body leaves our physical. All energetic lifeforms, entities, elementals, both negative and positive, exist in varying frequencies. Whatever is vibrating at a lower density is closer to our physical dimension. Higher realms resonate at a lesser density and are closer to the *Fifth-dimensional* rim.

I believe the topography and environment of each dimension is the direct result of its collective consciousness. Similarly, the collaboration of thoughts and emotions create energetic templates that draw to itself vibrational equivalents. Personally, I feel a lot safer in a city that's bright, clean and thriving over a dark and desolate one.

Women have told me that they can tell by a man's shoes how successful he is, and where he's going in life. What would happen if you frequently hung around negative people, and harboured negative emotions? What would you attract vibrationally? My dad always said, "You can tell a lot about a person by the company they keep." In regards to the astral world, just because it's the other side, it doesn't mean it's all good. My personal belief is that ouija boards attract dwellers from lower astral slums—darker entities pretending to be saints and loved ones.

The *Fifth dimension* is where time, duality and fear cannot exist. Their density is too low. Welcome to the kingdom of heaven, joy and unconditional love.

Is there anything beyond this dimension? I feel there are many more, yet who's to know? I believe there's more to be experienced vibrationally. This can be achieved by the process of ascension—raising your vibration.

## VIBRATION

*"If you want to find the secrets of the universe, think in terms of energy, frequency and vibration." ~ Nikola Tesla*

'In the beginning was the Word, and the Word was with God,' John 1:1 Gospel of John King James version. Then in Genesis 1:3 King James Bible 'And God said, Let there be Light: and there was Light.'

Could sound be turned into light to create matter? Can thoughts condense into physical manifestations? Nature may offer us some clues. Sonoluminescence is the phenomena of turning sound into light. Physicists noticed when the mantis shrimp snapped their claws, the speed of the jetting water produced cavitation. This is when water turns into bubbles, pull apart, and turn into a vapour. When the bubbles collapse onto themselves, they give off a quick snap, and light is produced. This light happens so fast it's barely noticeable. Turning light into matter was a process coined by Gregory Breit and John A. Wheeler in 1934. In 2014, physicists at Imperial College London came up with a way to physically demonstrate the Breit–Wheeler process. The photon-photon collider may be able to turn light into matter in the same way a gamma ray burst happens when a star collapses into a black hole. When two photons or light particles smash together, matter is created in the form of an electron and a positron. Science may be a long way off before proving this, but it doesn't mean it's not possible.

We exist in a sea of energy much like fish do in water. Like the fish, we are unaware of this permeating life force which is keeping us physically alive. There are many names for it: *Prana, Ki, Chi* and so forth. Our physical world appears real from our third-dimensional perspective. However, science tells us that everything is made up of empty space. Things feel solid because of an electric force. This force is dense, like our physical body. It contains similar amounts of negatively charged electrons and positivity charged protons. Behind all matter, is an energetic blueprint that sustains it. Frozen thoughts of scared geometrical shapes form the electro-skeleton. I believe this creative energy reacts to our thoughts and emotions.

You may have read about renowned Japanese researcher, Masaru Emoto. He discovered water changes in relation to the information it's given. He gave the water data, froze it, then photographed its crystals. Mr. Emoto would put water in vials and attach a label with written words on them such as love and hate. After they froze, he took photos of each droplet. To his surprise and after countless attempts, he noticed something miraculous. The water infused with love produced beautiful crystal formations. The water subjected to hate, fool, and other negative words produced incomplete and unpleasing crystal formations. Water is an element that is more sensitive to our thoughts than any other solid forms. If enough mental energy was directed to any substance, could we not be altered as well? The next time you hurl anger or hate toward yourself or another, keep in mind that we're made of mostly water. Blessing your food is not a message for the invisible God in the sky. No, it's to infuse it with love and gratitude—so it may be transformed.

Every thought and feeling you hold sets up a subtle vibration that oscillates. It expands and attracts similar resonating energy. If a tuning fork is calibrated to the key of C (432 Hz tuning), and a tone generator or instrument is set off to oscillate at the same cycle (16.05 Hz) the tuning fork would vibrate in unison. Our thoughts are electrical and our emotions are magnetic. When they merge, emotion is created. E-motion (electricity in motion) is a magnet that attracts similar frequencies to itself. The merging of thought and feeling creates a powerful electromagnet attraction. It is how the law of attraction works.

What we experience is a direct result of what we send out energetically. I often wondered how the great masters could materialize stuff out of thin air. To manifest in the *Third dimension* we are required to draw on the life force through thought, then infuse it with feeling, to create an emotion. Action is then needed to bring it into form. In the *Fourth dimension*, only thought and emotion is required. In the *Fifth dimension* only thought is needed. How cool would it be if we could manipulate matter just like a superhero? Why are children, and many adults, so fascinated by them? Perhaps, intuitively we know that we're capable of much more than we think we are. The closest I came to being a superhero was shattering a car window with intense emotion and focused thought.

I was in my father's car and he was driving. I would've been twenty at the time. We didn't always see eye to eye, and we'd argue a lot. One day, on the way to work we got into a heated discussion. It was about how stubborn and closed-minded he was. My father needs proof before he accepts anything as true. The argument escalated. I was so angry and yelled, "Anything could happen right now and you'd have no fucking clue why!" Everything in me wanted to show him that he was wrong. My rage boiled over! Almost immediately, his driver side window blew out and exploded to smithereens. Without saying a word, he stopped the car. His face was pale. In a low and shaky voice he said, "We've been shot." "Explain that!" I yelled, exhilarated. My euphoria then turned to fury. *What the fuck's it going to take for him to get it?* After a few hours had passed, I started to question what had happened. Did we get shot? Was I responsible, or was it a coincidence?

Why does it seem like some people have all the luck, while others appear to have a dark cloud that follows them wherever they go? Could it be caused by the thoughts that we keep thinking and believing? It doesn't matter if we're a good person or not—energy flows where it's directed.

We are transmitters and receivers of vibration, just like a tv and radio. We are free to send and receive any signal we want, positive or negative. When we turn on a radio, we'll hear whatever station the dial is set to. There are different bandwidths. The two most used are AM and FM. They range anywhere from 535-1605 KHz AM to 88-108 MHz FM. If you desire to listen to either the happy or sad broadcast, you'd simply move the dial. In the *Fourth dimension* it would be a piece of cake. The fact that we're in the *Third dimension*, means it's not as easy. This is why we get impatient and frustrated when things we want, don't happen right away.

The energetic density of the *Third dimension* slows everything down. Manifesting occurs gradually. It works more like a heating and cooling system, than that of a radio or tv. When we set the thermostat to a desired temperature, the system responds accordingly. If the thermostat is set to 68F/20C and the surrounding air temperature is colder, the heater kicks in and gradually warms to that setting. Conversely, if the temperature is hotter than what the thermostat is set to, the cooling system kicks in.

Changing our vibration can take time. Our thoughts and beliefs have to be in alignment. We attract what we're set to, not to what we want. The state of allowing speeds up the process, while resistance slows it down. To raise our vibration, we need to hold the intention and trust it will happen. It's not about forcing it—or mentally blowing out car windows.

## THE YOU'NIVERSE

*We are the universe—as above so below.*

What if our solar system was actually made of atoms from a larger universe? What if they are electrons rotating around a nucleus, like planets around the sun? What if our atoms are part of a smaller universe within us? Does it stop there?

Did you know that our brain's neural network looks identical to how dark matter is distributed in our galaxy? What if I told you that an eye looks like a nebula in space. That the creation of a human cell looks similar to when a star dies. Could it be possible? It's interesting to see that foods which are beneficial for certain body parts actually look similar: the brain looks like a walnut, celery resemble our bones, oranges have the appearance of mammaries—beets are good for our blood and so on.

We are all one—interconnected—anything is everything. There is no separation. We are part of a grand design. Our body is composed of the same elements as ancient stars, which have exploded eons ago. Scientists say that energy is never created or destroyed, it just changes form. Matter has forever retained the same mass, and always will. There is an algorithm to the universe, and it is not dictated by an egotistical man in the sky. It carries on, whether you pray to it or not, and it doesn't favour one person over another.

In Hinduism, there is a concept that God/Source Energy has three embodiments. They call it Trimurti, which means the trinity of God. The three facets are called: Brahma, Vishnu and Shiva. They represent: Creator, Preserver and Destroyer. If we look at these characteristics and what they symbolize, they imply that everything in creation is governed by these forces. Things are created, sustained and destroyed all at the same time. We are born, we live and we die. Our cells and all living things follow this same course. By the hand of time, rust, decay and corrosion devour everything. Nothing is permanent, all shall pass. This is why it's important we're not attached to anything, not even our physical body. We are not the flesh. We are spirit, and eternal.

Nature has a rhythm—it's cyclical—it is change. The cadence of the ocean's waves and the progression of the different seasons invite us to behold the Divine's cosmic dance. The only thing that doesn't change is change. Where there is resistance, there is struggle. Nature seeks balance. Allow it to unfold.

## KARMA

*'Every action has an equal and opposite reaction' ~ Sir Isaac Newton's third law of physics.*

On an energetic level, it's called karma. Some consider it to be the reaction of an angry and vengeful bitch. *Be not deceived; God is not mocked: for whatsoever a man soweth, that shall he also reap*, Galatians 6:7-8 of the King James version of the bible. This refers to all action, positive and negative. Energy has no bias. Every thought and action produces a ripple in the ether. It is like throwing a stone in to the water. The water ripples outward until it eventually returns like a boomerang. In Sanskrit, karma means action or doing. Every action you set in motion is stored. The displaced energy is stored in your DNA and energy body. It is uploaded into the akashic records much like a computer's hard-drive/cloud-storage system.

If you punch someone in the face, it's more than likely they will return the favour—action/reaction. If you punched yourself in the face you'd feel the pain immediately. If the person you pummelled didn't retaliate, the pain you inflicted is still owed to you, and you've incurred a karmic debt that you'll have to eventually pay off. The stored information will germinate at the appropriate time. It could happen immediately, or in another lifetime. It could be Rocco hired by your victim to come after you with a crowbar to bust your kneecaps. Or, you could be walking down the street and have a freezer accidentally fall on your head. You may call it bad luck, a freak accident, or years of planning by the person you punched. Sometimes it's an unknown messenger paying it forward. Maybe they were redeeming a credit owed to them incurred by another. Karma is not always tit for tat, it's an elaborate and collective barter system. It is far too complex to understand rationally.

One day I was at a petting zoo, feeding the goats. A bigger goat was stealing the food that I was giving to the baby. Upset, I spat on its face and told it to fuck off. Minutes later as I was walking back to my car, the lords of karma taught me about poetic justice. A bird shat on me. Not only did it manage to hit my face, but it landed on my eye and into my mouth. I was mad for a brief moment, until I realized the lesson. Sometimes karma is instant, and in this case it was. It was the last time I ever spat on anything.

In my teenage years, I worked as a stock boy at a building centre. I stocked shelves and helped customers take stuff to their car. I also drove a forklift in the shipping and receiving bay. Some days were boring as there wasn't much to do. Myself and a few other employees decided to cut the store's master-key. This allowed me to occasionally bring stuff home: a drill, a paint-sprayer and a ceiling fan. Definitely not a model red Ferrari. However, it was using the same payment method! It wasn't long before my parents house was broken into. All of my family's cherished valuables were stolen. My actions not only affected me, they affected my loved ones. From that day on, I no longer stole anything that didn't belong to me. I won't even buy stuff that I suspect has been ripped off. The debt incurred has to be paid off, eventually.

When people say they don't believe in God, it's usually followed by questioning an injustice. "How can He allow anyone to starve? How can He let innocent babies get raped?" I agree, and would find it hard to believe why, myself. What if reincarnation was true? What if these so called baby's were rapists and serial killers in their past lives? Wouldn't it make more sense if we did it to ourselves? A loving God would never do that, and wouldn't expect us to believe that it was His plan either. How would you feel if you knew Hitler was the baby that got raped?

Karma is not punishment. It is a system designed to teach us that we are all one. There's a common rule that every religion shares, "Do unto others as you would have them do unto you." What does this mean? When we harm another, we are harming ourselves. We are all connected. Until we grasp this, we will be stuck in duality.

## DUALITY (YIN & YANG)

Our physical world is governed by an energetic polarity called duality. There is no getting away from it while we're in physical form. This principle is represented by the Chinese symbol called Taijitu (Yin/Yang) an axiom derived from Taoism. It states, that all things manifested in the physical universe can not exist without its opposite condition. What this means is, there cannot be light without dark, cold without hot, happy without sad, and so forth. This doesn't suggest that these forces are opposing. In fact, they co-exist in harmony and complement one another. When they're separated, their equilibrium is disrupted and this causes tension. They are forever seeking their balance, and are constantly pursuing each other.

The *Yin Yang* symbol is contained within a circle. This represents all that exists in creation. One half is black and represents the feminine called *Yin*. This symbolizes: contraction, dark, cold, intuition, moon, soft and so on. The other half is white and represents the masculine called *Yang*. This symbolizes: expansion, light, hot, intellect, sun, hard and so on. In each other's half there is a dot of the opposing colour. This symbolizes the cycle of nature. It shows that a portion of the opposite condition is inherent in the other.'

*Every adversity, every failure, every heartache carries with it the seed of an equal or greater benefit' ~ Napoleon Hill.*

The desire to hold onto one state, such as happiness, causes tension. This magnetically pulls us toward a state of unhappiness. The intensity we use to pull apart something that inherently wants to remain whole, is equal to the force that pulls itself back. When we pull on an elastic band or push a swing, we're going to create tension. We cannot know happiness without the contrast of sadness. They are both one in the same. Both conditions are always present. Duality is just a varying degree of the same thing. The difference between Spock's Vulcan death grip and an enjoyable massage is only a matter of pressure. The more we hang onto one condition, the more we suffer, and the more we fear losing it. The solution is to step into the centre and honour both conditions. Allow all to be present, and let your awareness transcend them.

## GOOD AND EVIL

The illusion of good and evil is another concept that is based in duality. Could we be under a spell, where one is more favourable over the other? Religion/spirituality is built on the notion between the polarities of right and wrong. We're capable of being both the jerk and a goody-two-shoes. Each tenancy is inherent in us. Is the daytime considered better than the nighttime? One may be preferred and favourable over the other—that would depend if you were diurnal or nocturnal. Within the contrast lays the liberation and the imprisonment. One polarity will trap you, both will set you free. We say that evil is bad and that good is great. Have you considered that, the blackboard is required for us to see the white chalk? When our awareness expands beyond the confines of dualism, we realize the singularity. Pure unconditional love is an example, and is independent of any condition. With this awareness, duality doesn't exist. There are no opposites.

We understand that fear is the absence of love. We grasp that life is eternal, and is independent of birth and death. Light in its true essence is not binary, and does not cast a shadow. If you want to prove this, light a match and see if the flame casts one.

What if both religion and spirituality are a trap? A clever method of keeping us stuck in this game of life? Every good story has a powerful adversary, villain and dragon. Every plot narrates the defeat of the dark side. The story usually ends by embracing the light—the ultimate journey. What if this illusionary world was designed to keep us distracted? Could another game be set up beyond that of our current enslavement, one even more subtle? Many have moved away from religion, some shunning it altogether. Others have embraced it.

For most, our questions have outgrown the answers that religion is able to provide. Having unquestioning faith doesn't cut it anymore. The ancient texts were written thousands of years ago. They were scribed at a time when our collective conscious was at different level. Our comprehension is far greater today than it was then. Science has caught up, and less people are buying into outdated paradigms.

Even if we did transcend religion, media and consumerism. Despite the fact that we could conquer our addictions—there is always another level of deception ready to challenge us. Who is doing this? What is keeping us distracted and preventing us from becoming aware of our Divine power? The fight between good and evil has occurred for eons. Although the characters may have changed, it continues forever under the guise of duality. Could it be that both angels and demons work for the same team? The way to self-realization is not by avoiding the bad guys and following the good ones. Enlightenment is achieved by transcending the binary of dogma and realizing ourselves as the singularity. True evil is any entity, thought or action that perpetuates the delusion that we are separate from the omnipresent Divinity of Source Energy.

Hello my name is Frank, and I am a recovering Catho-holic. Forgive me father for what I'm about to say. Every Catholic funeral I've gone to was the same. The customs rarely differed. While attending a recent visitation I had an aha moment. The deceased was displayed in an open casket and dressed in a fine black suit. The priest talked about the Eucharist—it was Easter season. Then it dawned on me. Christianity has been mocked by the story of Dracula. Jesus said, "Whoever eats my flesh and drinks my blood has eternal life." Isn't that what Dracula does? I had to stop imagining that the corpse was going to reanimate. I had visions of him getting out of his coffin and biting the priests neck. In duality, the lines are always blurred.

## SPIRITUALITY AND RELIGION

*Religion is believing in another's experience, spirituality is believing in your own.*

The root word for religion comes from the two Latin words: re the prefix meaning return, and ligare meaning to bind. In other words, return to bondage or re-ligare. Authentic teachings show the transcendence of the twofold path. They lead us to the realization that we are ubiquitous. For me, the idea of being bound doesn't resonate to my concept of liberation.

I love the saying, 'Religion is for people not wanting to go to hell, and spirituality is for those who have already been there.' As you know, I was brought up Roman-Catholic as were most

Italians. I had to go to church every Sunday. It was never my thing, but I went because my mother strongly encouraged it. A Jewish friend once joked, "A Jew's guilt is inherited, and a Catholic's is learned."

In Mom's final days, my sister asked her if she wanted a Catholic funeral. Mom thought about it for a moment, paused and responded, "I think so... maybe I should, it was how I was raised." Boy, she had changed. It wasn't like I had never tried to convince her. I had, and would've preferred this version of her over the other. When my uncle and aunt got married, they decided to take a chance on a four-year old. As you know from my past, I wasn't the typical child at that age. Why they entrusted me as their ring-boy still remains a mystery. As soon as I saw the priest, I stopped dead in my tracks and the rings went flying. In absolute fear I ran and hid behind the pews.

I have studied every type of religion—I noticed most were rooted in patriarchy. God was always referred to as a dude. In Hinduism, they worship the Divine Mother. This made me think, was God a man or a woman, or neither? As you have already noticed, I'm not a big fan of religion. I believe that what we seek is found within the heart, through love, not hate. Imagine a world without religion—just simple observances felt in the heart.

*Do unto others as you want done unto you. Love others how you want be loved. Your body is the temple. The altar is your heart. Own every action without blame. Take responsibility for them, and without the expectation that another will redeem them.*

The only question you need to ask yourself is, "Am I in love, or am I in fear?" It has been said that actions speak louder than words. If this is true, then be love. Real sin is born from ignorance, and from the fear that we're separate from Source energy. In every one of us there is a longing to remember our greatness. We set off on this journey agreeing to forget it all. Only a faint memory of it remains. Our soul is constantly coaxing us back into remembering. All the answers are within us. Unfortunately, we've been taught to look outside ourselves.

## AN OLD HINDU LEGEND

Once upon a time, all human beings were gods. They were all equally powerful, but they misused their Divinity. So Brahma, the main God, decided to take it away from them and hide it where it could never be found. Brahma called on his council of gods to help him decide where to hide it. "Let's bury it deep within the Earth," said one of the gods. But Brahma answered, "No, that will not do, humans will eventually dig into the earth and find it." "Let's sink it into the deepest ocean," said another. Again Brahma said, "No, for one day humans will learn how to dive and they will find it." "On top of the highest mountain," said another. Once again Brahma said, "This will not do, for one day they will climb every mountain and certainly find it."

The gods gave up and said, "If humans will eventually find all the places on the Earth, where will you hide it?" After some thought Brahma said, "We will hide their Divinity in the place where no human will ever think to look." "Where is that?" they asked. Brahma's response, "It will be hidden deep within the centre of their own being. They'll never look there." Ever since the deed was done, humans have been searching all over Earth for something already within themselves.

Religion and suffering are like a boat. Once your cross over the water to the other side, they are no longer needed.

# CHAPTER EIGHT

# THE RIVER

*"They didn't realize, all those years ago. The pain they caused,
and the tears that flowed, let them go." Excerpt from the song
'Little child' 2016 by Frank Di Genova*

Row, row, row your boat,
Gently down the stream.
Merrily, merrily, merrily, merrily,
Life is but a dream.

In Greek mythology there are many rivers flowing in the Underworld. The river Styx is perhaps the most popular. It represents hate, and is the one that separates the land of the living from the realm of the dead. There are two springs at its entrance, each with opposing characteristics. Lethe is the river of forgetfulness—drinking from it causes complete loss of memory. Mnemosyne is the river of remembrance—drinking from it brings back all memory and restores one's omniscience. The ancients believed when one died and crossed into the Underworld, they would be given a choice. Drink from Lethe, and forget all you've learned and be reborn, or drink from Mnemosyne and forever be in joy. Which river would you desire to drink from?

I was visiting with a good friend who had travelled and lived in India for six years. He was telling me of the time he had spent on the sacred mountain of Kailash in Tibet. There, lies a river called the Indus—it's one of the longest in Asia. He said he could jump from one bank to the other at its origin because it's so narrow and shallow. Yet, this river grows to three thousand two hundred km in length and is over one thousand kilometres squared at is basin. It passes through India, Pakistan and China, and discharges into the Arabian sea.

Rivers are usually formed and fed from melting glaciers. They are created by springs, rainwater and by underwater streams. The freshwater flows downhill as a trickle at first, then swells into a stream. It then joins with other side streams, called tributaries which get wider and stronger until it becomes a river. As the water flows, it collects rocks, stones and other material. This is called the river's load. It etches, winds and widens the landscape, eating everything in its path—even solid rock. The river's speed and flow increases, and gets stronger, until it eventually finds its way back to the sea.

As my friend was sharing his experience, a clear vision came to me. Our life is like a river, in so many ways. The beginning is called the Source. The next part is called the youthful river. Then the mature river follows, and like a teenager, moves wild and fast. Further down, the old river slows considerably and empties into the sea—waiting to be reborn once again. There are forks that represent the many choices and directions we choose to take in life. Sometimes our life feels like the waterfalls and rapids that move fast and uncontrollable. At times the rocks and dams slow us down. They give us time to integrate and recharge as we tread water. We meet others along the way, much like twigs and branches that attach and detach. Sometimes they float together only for a short distance, while at other times they stick together until the river meets the sea.

A river is an analogy for how our thoughts create our reality. We can be in flow, or in resistance. At its headwater, a river starts off as a drip—similar to an idea. The idea becomes a wish and the drip trickles faster, turning into a helpless desire. The trickle then becomes a stream that turns into a stronger wish. As our desire grows, it turns into an intention. Like tributaries, these intentions join together and gain strength. As the force becomes even stronger, the intention turns into determination. At this point, it's so strong that it can carve through solid rock. This unstoppable load is akin to a person with an unrelenting volition—ultimate willpower. As is with all things, a small idea can turn into something incredibly big and powerful. The grand oak tree was once a small acorn.

Have you ever made a paper boat and floated it downstream? Have you watched the way leaves float along the gutters of a road after heavy rainfall? Were you fascinated at how quickly the current carried the leaves? Did you notice how effortlessly they floated without resistance? Sometimes they might catch something and slow down, or even stop—just for a moment. As a child I used to love making tin foil boats and race them down a stream or my street's curb. I enjoyed watching them float on the current—until boredom set in. I'd throw rocks or try to sink them with a slingshot. Looking back it was evident and indicative of a pattern. My dreams were submerged, and I was sabotaging my goals. Where might those little ships have landed, had I let them go? What adventures awaited?

## BLOCKING THE FLOW

Like the blood in our veins and air in a room, water is energy and needs to flow and circulate. When an element is obstructed resistance builds. If the flow stops, stagnation occurs. Thoughts and actions are no different. They too can become static. What happens to water if it sits for a long period of time? It becomes stale, foul smelling and murky. Unpleasant things can start to grow in it, until eventually the life force withdraws. What if we lived our life resisting it? How many of us do? Are you allowing your life to flow like a river? Or are you putting up dams? Are you pushing the river? Is it causing irritability and impatience? Did you know that any pain or disease you experience in your body, is caused by some type of resistance?

In my high school electronics class I loved blowing things up real good. When the teacher left the classroom, which was often, I'd hook up a resister to a controlled power source, raise the voltage and fry it. I can't believe he never commented on the smell when he returned. Resistors are electronic components that reduce the current flow in a circuit. If the current is too high, the resistors will overload and blow. Moral of the story... I liked to blow shit up. On a serious note, I've learned that pushing or resisting life only causes discomfort. When we allow it to circulate, life flows effortlessly. If we don't, we may blow a fuse.

I was on my way to visit my acupuncturist, (the man who cured my facial neuralgia) and traffic wasn't co-operating. I was late for my first appointment. In a panic I called him, "Dr. I'm stuck in traffic, I'll get there soon." His response was brilliant, "No go fast—no go slow—go the same." It reminded me of the mantra I used to say during my crazy teenage days. *"Go with the flow!"* That got me out of so many jams. I wonder why I stopped using it?

I ushered in this chapter with a famous nursery rhyme. I felt it was the perfect analogy of how to live life (a dream). How do you row your boat? Does it have an Evinrude V8 engine, or do you use oars? Is it a fishing boat, paddle boat, or a canoe? Do you burn up and down the lake? Or, do you float peacefully with the current? When we resist the flow of life, we're not trusting. Instead, we force and impose our will. You can't stop its current, it's going to keep flowing. Just like a wave in the ocean—try stopping one.

The more we resist, the more pain and dis-ease we experience. The trouble is many of us are conditioned to think that we need to suffer, and struggle to achieve anything worthwhile. Where has that gotten anyone? Probably sick and tired, physically, mentally and emotionally. Do you know how much water pressure is at the base of the Hoover Dam in Nevada? It can be up to forty-five thousand pounds per square foot. That is a lot of tension. Can you imagine the pressure if it sprung a leak? The next time you feel tension brewing inside you, be it resistance, fear or anger, remember how much force the dam is blocking. You are the river and the river is inside you—let it flow. Let go and *pay* attention to the river *bank*, let your joy be your *current/sea* (currency). We're not here to drift through life. We're here to set forth our intentions and allow them to flow and unfold.

## DAMN YOU

The dams we create by our resistance manifest in many different forms. When we feel anger, fear or anxiety, we usually tense our body. When we do, we trap energy and block its flow. This creates stagnation, which causes density, and inflammation to occur. I tend to carry stress in my lower back, and hold onto worry in my stomach. This results in belly bloat and back pain.

Energy moves like water. It flows freely and takes the path of least resistance. This notion is found in the Chinese philosophical system called Feng Shui—meaning wind-water. The wind is the carrier of *Qi* (life force/energy/Ki) and the water is the accumulator. Our body is such a carrier. Our veins, nerves and organs transport blood, electrical nerve signals and life force throughout our system. Acupressure points called meridians, axiatonal lines and chakras are also conduits of energy. They exist at a higher vibration where we cannot physically see with our eyes.

Whenever we experience shock, or upheaval of any kind, it's energetically encoded as a memory in our cells and organs. If we don't release it, our subconscious will recreate the experience exponentially until we pay attention. The more we ignore it, the more pain and discomfort we feel. The only thing that will go away by ignoring it, is our teeth (they will fall out if we neglect them). If your spouse is nagging you a lot, maybe it's time to pay attention. The same is true with any type of resistance or denial. We can try to deflect it as much as we want, but eventually we won't be able to. It will keep coming until we face it. We may change jobs, partners or move to the other side of the globe, but whatever pain we're ignoring will keep surfacing. Circumstances will continue triggering us until we finally pay attention. The consequences of not releasing these experiences is we will self-destruct. When energy can't flow effortlessly through an organ—let's say the liver—stagnation occurs and builds up pressure like a dam. As the energy densifies, the organ starts to deteriorate. The more it deteriorates, the weaker the vibration, until it eventually dies.

In Chinese medicine organs are associated with emotions. Staying with my example of the liver, this correlates with anger. If we were to hang on to this low vibration of anger, it would eventually attack our liver and cause it to become weak. Hepatitis and cirrhosis could occur. I believe my liver was angry at me for being angry. *Sorry for drowning you with all that alcohol.*

We are led to believe that if we don't address an emotion or experience, it will disappear. Well, this is true if there's no longer an emotional attachment to it. Most of us are in denial and pretend that we're free of its affect. So where does it go? Our body is a barometer of our mental and emotional states. Our biology is composed of the stories we keep telling and identifying with. Some think when we get sick, it's the luck of the draw. How many times do we hear of a healthy person who never drank or smoked, yet dropped dead at forty-five? Health and lifestyle are very important, but not as much as our internal wellbeing is. Stress is the silent killer.

## WATER

Water is life. It sustains us, and is abundant. Without it, we will die. Our body is made up of a high percentage of water—a similar percentage covers the Earth. Symbolically, water represents emotions in dream analysis. This is also true when we cry or laugh very hard—tears flow. Water can be a purifier or a destroyer. This is depicted in many beliefs and cultures. For example, in India the great Ganges River is where spiritual devotees bathe to cleanse themselves of their sins and wrongdoings. In many religions, baptism is considered sacred and is used for cleansing and purifying—symbolic of rebirth. Moses parting the sea and the building of Noah's Ark in the great flood, represent the preservation and renewal of life. Water smoothes out jagged rocks and cleanses rivers of stagnant particles. Running water creates relaxing sounds, and provide healing benefits of negative ions. We influence water, as it also effects us. That's why it's important to be mindful of our thoughts. When we bathe or shower, it becomes a sacred act when we turn it into a ritual, by being conscious of cleansing and purifying our body and mind. When making an infused beverage, and we instil love into the liquid we are raising its vibration—we are honouring what we are ingesting into our body.

Water is a carrier of energy. It creates sound when it moves—from the soothing trickles of the fountain and stream—to the majestic roar of a waterfall. Have you ever heard the cosmic sound of Om? Not while chanting it, but the actual cosmic sound. It can be heard while in deep meditation, when the mind is quiet. It sounds like a large waterfall. When I was at Niagara Falls, Canada and sitting by the overhang, I heard it. The sound was incredible—beyond words. The next time you're there, close your eyes and listen.

The Bible explains this in Revelation 14:2 (King James Version) "*And I heard a voice from heaven, as the voice of many waters, and as the voice of a great thunder: and I heard the voice of harpers harping with their harps.*"

## A DROP IN TIME

'Time is an illusion' ~ Albert Einstein.

Our lives pass through time, much like a river does—life doesn't stop. Time is a linear measurement in which events can be ordered, in the sequence of past, present and future. It is the duration between these events. It separates the present moment into then and when. But, it's always the present moment. When you place your hand in flowing water, the water you feel passing is never the same. Your hand is still and is in the now moment. The passing water represents the passing of time. You can relate this to the light source that passes through the lens of an old film projector. We are the light, the timeless and of non-physical form. The film passing through represents time and life events. Time can be frozen with pictures and recordings. Yet, it cannot be isolated. The ripples of thought distort the perception of our true nature, as timeless beings. We exist in all time, and in no time. This concept is difficult to grasp because we're using a time-based faculty (the mind) to identify something that can't be comprehended.

My son's wisdom shone brightly at the early age of three. I was studying Buddhism and decided to ask him what he thought time was. "Luke, what time is it buddy?" He responded quickly and without thinking. "It's now daddy." What could I say to that? He was right. My only concern was that men in red robes might come knock on my door and ask to interview him. It's a shame we lose our inner Buddha to the mind and its perceptions.

## LEAF IT ALONE

The following is a simple meditation for calming the mind and relaxing the body. Make sure you won't be disturbed for at least fifteen minutes. Turn off your cell phone and other electronic devices so you are not interrupted.

Thoughts will come and attempt to engage you. One cannot stop them from surfacing. The secret is not to engage, just watch them pass without judgment. Do this by allowing them to float by like leaves do on a river. Some find it helpful to imagine a flowing river and watch each leaf, as a thought, drifting by. The mind loves to be engaged, and it won't stop looking for things to get caught up in. By witnessing the sound of our breath, we are giving it a task. This will be enough to distract the mind from attaching to thoughts. It will take time to train your mind, yet don't fret if you don't feel you're successful the first time you do it. Keep practicing. The more you do, the easier it will become.

Sit in a comfortable chair with your back straight, feet flat on the floor. Keeping your head level, place your hands on your lap with your palms facing up. Make sure your shoulders are back and not slouching forward. Close your eyes and take three deep slow breaths. Hold the breath slightly at each end of the inhale and exhale. If you can, breathe in through the nose and out through the mouth. Otherwise, breathe in and out through the nose. If you have any nasal obstruction then do so entirely from your mouth. Breathe as naturally as you can and without forcing your breath. Just observe it. Listen to the sound of your breath naturally flowing in and out, until you feel at one with its cycle. Let the breath breathe you.

## THE RIVER MEDITATION

Have someone read this to you while you are visualizing the guided meditation, or you can record it and play it back. It is available on my website as a free download at www.frankdigenova.com

Get into a comfortable position and close your eyes. Begin with the *leaf it alone* meditation, then take a deep breath in through your nose and hold slightly, to centre yourself. As you exhale, feel a wave of warm relaxation flow slowly over your entire body—from your head to your toes. See yourself walking along a winding path in a lush green pasture. You notice a small hill ahead and move toward it. You start to climb and notice colourful wildflowers nestled along the path. At the top, a thick dense forest comes into view. As you make your way down the hill, feel the soft cool grass beneath your feet. You can hear the sound of water flowing, and birds chirping in the trees ahead. Follow the path slopping down, where you will see a flowing river. Feel the pebbles crunch beneath your feet as you walk over them. Make your way to the edge of the river.

Look along the bank and see the slender tress bending over the water—rocks and rich brown mud is settled along the river's edge. You notice the swirls and how they reflect sunlight off the clear water as it flows. A small raft is tied to a tree. Sturdy and made from smooth solid wood, you untie the rope and get on. Gently, you push away from the bank. A wave of warmth envelopes your body as you drift down the river.

Feel the gentle rise and fall of the river waves. Become aware of the soft rocking motion as you drift. Listen to the gentle slapping of the water against the sides of the raft. You are totally relaxed. Feel the warm sun kissing your skin, his rays permeating your entire being with calming energy. Smell the fresh scents of the water and lush grass. A gentle breeze passes by. Allow all your senses to absorb your surroundings with every cell in your body.

Look over the side of the raft and see all the different coloured fish swimming beneath you, darting here and there. You see red fish... orange... and yellow. With each colour you see, your body fills with passion and creativity. A large green fish stops and looks right at you. You feel safe, connected—and filled with love. Look up. Notice the clear blue sky and fluffy clouds. Birds move in the branches above you. Their cheerful chirps celebrate your presence. Close your eyes and let your intuition guide the raft along the river... when it comes to a stop, open your eyes.

Tall lush trees stand ahead of you. You step out of the raft and onto the sandy shore. It is warm beneath your feet. The sun is setting in the sky and you behold a beautiful sunset. Walk towards a large rock, climb it, and sit on it. Instantly, you feel grounded and connected to the earth. Fertile soil surrounds the stone chair. It's dark and rich, and you can smell its earthy perfume. Breathe this into the centre of your being and feel your heart warm, glowing with an emerald light. You notice little seedlings sprouting from the soil.

A carpet of green stems bend toward you, pulled to the love you are emanating, and burst into colour. Blooming into purple, pink and violet flowers, each blossom produces a seed and offers it to you. They thank you for the gift you have given them—your light—that has initiated their growth. In return, their seeds are for your growth. Carry these seeds and know all the wisdom that is needed for your new journey is contained within them. You bow in gratitude for this Divine exchange. Be still and allow the seeds to germinate within you.

The time has come to leave. You climb down the rock and make your way across the sandy shore to the raft. It appears larger than it was before. As you board the raft you notice it's now twice the size. You push away from the shore and float down the river once again.

Feel connected to Mother Earth and all of her beings—feel the oneness... the peace... and balance. Your raft brings you to the entrance of a beautiful Grotto. Inside is dim. Yet, as you enter, the water shines a crystal blue and the stone walls shimmer as if inlaid with glistening diamonds. You are in Mother Nature's womb, ready to be reborn. Enjoy the stillness, feel nurtured and know all is well. Several moments pass until the raft starts moving again. The passage out is ahead. As you move through, you are consumed with absolute bliss—you have consciously been reborn. Flow with the gentle current, feeling renewed and totally relaxed...

The river takes you back to where you started. It looks different, yet the same. It is you that has changed. Climb with ease off the raft. Slowly begin your walk back... over the hill... across the green pasture... and to where you began your journey on the winding path.

It is time to come back to the here and now. You feel refreshed and deeply peaceful, you have attained more wisdom. Love permeates your entire being. Focus your attention on your breath... and gently come back...

You will hear the numbers one to five. Slowly and with each breath, your awareness of the present moment comes back into focus. Wiggle your toes and gently wake the rest of your body. Open your eyes and become aware of where you are. Take a few deep breaths, and stretch your body.

We are the river and the river is us—let it flow. When we stop resisting, we enjoy the ride and experience its ebb and flow—its cascades and dribbles. We are not meant to build dams, canals and lodges like the beaver does. Nor are we like the salmon that swims up stream to spawn, only to die and become food for nearby predators. Miracles happen, when we allow the flow of water to quench the ignorance and fear, that has parched our oasis into a desert.

I used to block the flow of life by paddling my boat against its current. The boat was my body. It was tired and stressed—it was leaking. I was sinking.

# CHAPTER NINE

# Why It's Hard To Change

*"Why's it hard to see? What it takes to be a man? What it takes to understand? And how to live life happy everyday? Excerpt from the song 'Why?' 2007 by Frank Di Genova*

As a child, my parents used to visit friends and relatives often—I never wanted to go. I would kick and scream and plead to stay home, but they always won. At first it was awkward, but after we got past the initial hellos, I settled in and was fine. When it came time to leave, I didn't want to go! The ego works in the same way. When it encounters something new, it resists. Then, as it becomes familiar with the situation, and the guard is let down, it feels safe. It becomes so comfortable that it won't want to part with it—until the cycle begins again. This is why change can sometimes take time.

How do we focus on any one thing when our thoughts are restless and feral? How is this possible when our mind is filled with drunk little monkeys all clamouring for attention? Where and how do we start a new healthy food habit when our body is addicted to stimulants such as sugar, salt, fat, caffeine and alcohol? Are we really able to change our behaviour when we're fixated on the past or worried about the future? How does one change when they continue to hide behind the stories and excuses that they keep perpetuating? Are we secretly waiting for that magic hand in the sky to come save us? Some of us feel that we've suffered enough and have earned the right for redemption. Is this you? Do you feel that it's owed to you? How do we change when we're slaves to our senses, and are afflicted with fear and bad habits? How can we reshape our life if we don't believe it's possible?

There is no use in trying to start any program, meditation, healthy eating regime, or discipline without first preparing the mind and body beforehand. How many times have you tried and failed? No. You're not weak. You're just not aware of how to go about it. Sometimes we need someone who's been through it to show us. I've read many books on *how-to*, and each time I've attempted to follow their suggestions, I have failed. I don't remember any of them mentioning that we have to prepare our body, and change our belief system first. Or, it could be that I only sought the magic formula and looked past the words. Maybe I wasn't ready to integrate them. The most effective way to achieve lasting change is to remove everything that is preventing us from doing so. This means removing toxins from our body on all levels: physically, mentally and emotionally. We need to understand why we desire the change. Once we do, the next step is to alter our limiting beliefs into empowering ones. We can affirm all the positive feel-good jargon we like, be diligent in our approach, yet nothing will change unless we attend to our core beliefs. What often results are feelings of frustration, defeat, and unworthiness.

## COMFORT ZONE

While all the things you want are outside your comfort zone, everything you have now is within. When a ripe fruit sits for too long, it starts to rot. It's the same with stagnant water, air, and energy/life force. Everything needs to keep circulating, growing and expanding.

Our habits, thoughts and actions are stored inside our subconscious mind. They are ingrained into our brain like grooves in a record. These neurological pathways are etched in the same way that we walk through the woods or over grassy fields. Each time we plod over the same terrain we pack it down just a little more—until eventually, a path is made. This is how we learn a new skill, or implant a new habit. This can be a good thing, although not when we want to break a bad (or negative) habit. By keeping things new and fresh, it makes it harder to get stuck in a rut. It is like our footprints in the sand being washed away by the waves.

We are creatures of habit and prefer to stay in a state of comfort. Whenever we attempt to do something different, our subconscious mind causes us discomfort—both physically and emotionally. Our subconscious is well aware of our comfort zone, and does whatever it can to keep us there. It is programmed to keep us safe. The little voice we hear is an obedient servant. It does its job, maybe too well, as it draws on our collection of past memories, and the fear of our future. You've heard it before, "No that's too hard. It's no use. All that effort. You'll hurt tomorrow. Stay on the couch. Better not say how I feel, I can't afford to get fired. What if they say no?" Sound familiar? Our little voice can be a procrastinator. Mine seemed to enjoy postponing things. It loved whispering, "Tomorrow, or wait till Monday." My father said that as a child I would often say, "Domani Papa." Can you guess what it means in English?

My inner voice convinced me that he was my best buddy—that was until I called him on his bullshit. He masqueraded as my intuition. But I learned how to catch him in the act. Now whenever I feel fear, I know it's him and not my intuition. A true friend empowers you and gets you to take action. They tell you to ask the guy/girl out, and not to take it personally if they say no.

I used to moan at the thought of doing exercise. I'd rather sit on the couch and crush a bag of chips while I watched tv. The thought of doing cardio and lifting weights made me want to stay on the couch even more. I never thought to ask myself, *"What's worse, the pain and discomfort of exercising, or not being able breathe and fit into my clothes?"*

As we break through our comfort zone we expand. We gain knowledge, acclimatize and become stronger. We're able to take on more challenges, experience new things, and start really living life to its fullest. Our desire has to be greater than the pain and fear of not having what we want—and greater than our fear of, *what if?* If we truly want something, we will find a way. If not, we'll find excuses. There is a saying that what we seek is on the other side of our fear. See you on the other side.

## SILVER PLATTER

*'Good timber does not grow with ease, the stronger the wind, the stronger the trees.' ~ Douglas Malloch.'*

Being in flow is not expecting everything to come easy. The seedling needs to be hardened off before it's planted. The resort I stayed in on my honeymoon had an in-house casino. The only other place I knew where to gamble was at Lost Wages (Las Vegas). This would be my first time gambling, aside from the marriage vows I took just days before. Slot machines were ready to take my money. They did, fifty dollars in fifteen minutes. That was the first and last time a one arm bandit, or any game of chance took my money. I wonder, *"If I had won, would I have continued to gamble?"* Bill Gates once stated, 'Success is a lousy teacher. It seduces smart people into thinking they can't lose.'

I believe failure is a better teacher than instant success. When things come too easily, it gives us a false sense that it should always be easy. My fear of failing in school was a strong motivator for me to do my best—although that wasn't always the case. Thankfully, I never failed a grade. Today, the fear of failing has lessened. I'm not saying we must suffer to have a sense of success, however, embracing challenge does strengthen us. When we lift weights, the resistance builds our muscles. Generally, we tend to focus on the goal rather than the process of getting there. Trophies, medals and ribbons are commemorative ways of symbolizing an accomplishment—it's not the goal. The journey is what's important. It's what you become during the process of achieving it. Wouldn't it get boring if we always got everything we wanted? Just ask any woman who has ever had a yes-man in her life. How can anything be appreciated if it's not earned?

I was a spoiled brat growing up. It was awesome at the time, but it didn't prepare me for the challenges life had in store. It was hard adjusting at first, as there was no one there to bail me out when things got heavy. Spoiling me was how my parents showed their love. I don't blame them at all. I'm actually grateful. This realization, though, led me to parent Luke in a different way—although I was still overprotective. I wanted him to learn on his own and experience things. When he failed, I wasn't hard on him—he learned. He always knew that I was there for him, if and when he needed. Biblically, the whole idea of not succumbing to temptation is a perfect example. It explains how we get stronger by not giving in—and weaker when we do.

## SABOTAGE

My friends kept telling me how talented, smart and funny I was. They never understood why I was so unhappy and struggling. One of my best friends would often get mad at me by saying, "I don't know anyone who has as much potential as you, piss it all away!" He would share stories with others of how I masterfully captivated people with my charm and charisma—especially with groups of women. I admit, I loved hearing it, and would relive the experiences vicariously through his narrative. I knew I was that person, yet, at the same time didn't believe it. Instead I hid myself away. My camouflage was getting drunk. I used humour, excuses and procrastinated. The underlying cause—I feared my power. I got fat to protect myself from being vulnerable, and emotionally and physically available. Who would love a guy with a fat gut? I often felt alone and depressed—it was a vicious cycle.

I ended my relationships before things got too serious. Or, I offered the 'friends with benefits' option. Either way, I'd treat my woman as if they were my beloved. I'd kiss them on their forehead, and cater to their every need. They were given mixed signals. I wanted their approval, their love, but without getting too deep. At that point in my life, even if the perfect woman appeared, I would find something wrong with her. I would find an excuse not to move forward.

When I did try to claim my worth, I went all out. It was extreme and hardcore. I did two twelve-week body challenges over eleven years—shedding forty-pounds each time. It worked for a bit, I got the attention I wanted and it felt good. It wasn't long, though, before I started to sabotage myself again—going deeper and further into despair. There was always an excuse that prevented me from taking charge of my life. There's not enough time. Or, I wasn't ready. Sadly, deep down, I didn't want to be alive. My mantra had become, "Ya but."

There was a reason why I never learned full songs on the guitar. It was so I wouldn't have to play in front of anyone. If I did, I'd make sure I was drunk and that people knew. My mistakes were then because of the booze and not because I sucked. Being drunk also helped numb my anxiety of being on the spot. The songs I wrote were never finished—they had to be perfect.

Hiding, procrastinating, perfection and self-sabotage were my middle names. My expectations were unrealistic, and would never be met.

I used any excuse not to stand in my power. I didn't want to be judged, or to fuck up. Whenever I was successful, I got scared. Being afraid of my power meant I shut it off. If I didn't try, I couldn't fail, right? I was afraid of success, and hated being a failure.

## PANHANDLER

Every now and then a new street person would claim the famous corner close to the salon. It was Mike's turn, and it didn't take long before we started sharing hellos and goodbyes. We all want to be acknowledged regardless of our social status, that's why I make a point to acknowledge everyone—even if it's just a smile.

One of our clients was making a documentary and chose our resident panhandler for his story. Part of the narrative was Mike getting his haircut. The cameras rolled in the salon as he was filmed. In addition to his pre-paid haircut, Mike was given a whack of cash and relocated for rehabilitation. It was a feel-good story. Nonetheless, I had my doubts.

Two months later I walked past the famous corner and was welcomed with a familiar greeting. "Hey Frank... ha ha ha," I said, "Hey Mike, what happened?" "Well... I don't know, ah... I was on the train and then, you know... I had all this money and... something in me snapped... I went to Winnipeg instead... lost the cash and now I'm back here." I laughed inside, knowing he would be back. Our good samaritan, the filmmaker client, was mortified.

## SELF-PUNISHMENT

Maybe I knew Mike was going to vandalize his chance for help because it was something I was doing to myself everyday. I was a walking time bomb, and ready to explode at any moment. My health wasn't the best, and I ate shit food and didn't care. I wasn't smoking two packs of cigarettes anymore, but I drank and ate junk food daily. I was a walking inferno of emotional and physical inflammation, constantly tired and bloated. It was time for me to make healthier choices. But how? I was a vegetarian for seven years, worked out religiously, and did everything I could to gain control of my life. But yet, I fell short.

At one point, I was drinking six large cups of coffee a day. My day ended with a triple-espresso and a nightcap. I would take a glass of vodka or cognac with me to bed. By morning the glass would often be empty. Sometimes, it would be knocked over and its contents were spilled to the floor. My emotions were also out of control—angry, depressed and irritable, I was a mess. I am grateful to be here and share my story with you. I believe that we endure things for a reason.

Many called me an extremist, and they were right. Whenever I did anything, it was full boar or nothing at all. The concept of moderation and balance was foreign to me. So was the idea of a lifestyle change. I must have been a yogi or a monk in a past life, because my ability for abstinence is off the charts. I could accomplish anything that I put my mind to. The problem was, after my great feats were completed, I thought my job was done. It didn't last, and that's when I'd come undone. It was back to my regular programming. It didn't take long for me to return to the starting line. Often, it was further back. Who was I kidding? Every time I failed, my confidence went deeper into despair.

There has always been a struggle within me—a tug of war. The perfect example of extremes was the spiritual guy versus the party animal. Both hid from the other. I was Dr. Jekyll and Mr. Hyde (hide). How could anyone take me seriously or follow my example? I was the do what I say guy, and not what I do guy—a hypocrite. I was sick and tired of being sick and tired. I resolved to finally get my shit together. I had to align my thoughts, emotions, actions and what I ate, and forge them into one synergy. My approach was to address them all as a totality instead of compartmentalizing each aspect separately. I knew all the parts so well, but didn't know how to integrate them as a whole.

## CLARITY

You have to know what you want in order to get it. Yet, most of us don't have a clue—clarity is everything. In addition, we need to know why we want something. With enough why's that are clarified, anything can be accomplished. What's most important, is to be aware that whatever you seek is not the end-game. It is not the panacea of all that ails you. With every goal that I attained, an empty promise followed. None lived up to their pledge, or my expectation of being satiated—nothing filled the void. It was false advertisement. Spirituality states that happiness is not found through material things. Yet, I found no happiness through spirituality. I was screwed, there was no way of winning. There had to be a way out of this. How could I live consciously and not have the repo-man confiscating my stuff? I had to make a plan.

## PLAN

The plan has to be realistic and achievable. What we want isn't always what's best for us. Sometimes, better things are in store. We need to be flexible and adapt to whatever arises. Write down your intents, goals and why you want them. Next, answer how you'll realistically achieve them. Be specific. Let's say you want to lose twenty pounds. If your goal is to lose them in then next two weeks, you're not being realistic—you'll fail. Instead, write down, I am going to lose twenty pounds over the next four months. I am going to stop eating and drinking junk food. I am going to exercise three times a week and so forth. It has to be attainable and sustainable. Read your plan daily so it sinks into your subconscious—charge it with e-motion (electricity in motion). Eventually, the drip will turn into a gushing rapid, and you will become a powerful electromagnet. Things will start happening.

## KNOWLEDGE IS NOT POWER

Successful people have no problem sharing the knowledge they have. Unsuccessful people horde anything they come across and guard it, like it was the Arc of the Covenant. Why do you think that is? Most believe that knowledge is power, it's not. We literally have the world at our fingertips. Anyone with a computer and access to the internet, with a few keystrokes, can answer every question within seconds. This doesn't make you smarter. Actually, it levels the playing field. The guy giving away the free information knows that less than ten percent of the people listening will actually take action. I was part of the ninety percent. I was ignorant and thought I knew it all. Why was he giving away free information? What was his motive? It's funny how we blindly accept mass media bullshit. Yet, when we hear something that may benefit us, we put up our guard.

How many of us are unhappy? How many of us pretend that we have life all figured out? How many of us blame the system for all the things that are screwed up in the world? Why don't we walk our talk? Why do we complain about what's wrong, but never do anything about it?

Knowledge isn't power, action with knowledge is. Most of the things I have written about in this book, I knew long ago, but never applied them. There is a difference between understanding something and knowing it. One is on a mental level, and the other is on a soul level. Things started changing only when I took action and applied what I knew. Whatever you read in these pages are just words that are strung together—arrows pointing to ideas. Positive thinking without positive action will get you positively nothing—except disillusion. It's like locking yourself in a room while your praying to God asking for a miracle. If you're stuck inside, how will it happen? How long have you been waiting?

There seems to be a know-it-all in every family, work place, and group of friends. They act like they know everything and have an answer for every problem. They're all talk and no action. These armchair coaches are typically lazy and don't do a thing, yet they're the first ones to tell you what you're doing wrong. They'll discourage you, put you down and call you crazy. It's mostly the case when you're doing something that they were too afraid to try themselves. They are the first to brag and will always try to one-up you. My adage is, if they're not living it, they're full of shit! Actions speak louder than words.

## FOCUS & PERSISTENCE

We are so used to getting instant rewards. Technology has allowed us to expect things immediately. Email, texts, drive-thru's, and on-demand tv shows, are at our beck and call—literally with a push of a button. We're possessed, restless and plagued by a sense of entitlement. I feel it's safe to say that we are all guilty on some measure of impatience.

I remember teaching Luke to play a tune on the guitar. He had never played a guitar before. I was in awe as it had taken me days to learn what he did on his first try. I went out and bought him a mini Stratocaster-clone with a practice amp. My son was a virtuoso. The days turned into weeks and he played daily—only it wasn't on the Fender, it was with Guitar Hero. I asked, "Luke, why aren't you playing the guitar I bought you?" "Dad, this is more fun, and playing a real guitar is hard." I said, "Luke, if it was easy everyone would do it. Doing stuff that's hard is what makes a person accomplish great things in life." I didn't push. I knew if he loved it enough, he would continue without my prodding.

The moment I heard Eddie Van Halen play Eruption, I knew I had to learn to play the guitar. My best friend and I signed up for lessons. My father was always on me to practise, but it became a chore. I wanted to rock, not play Red River Valley. I would do anything to get out of practising—recording these sessions with my tape-deck and playing them back, so he'd think I was playing. I was a few weeks ahead in Mel Bay's workbook than my friend was, and my ego got the best of me. I was convinced lessons were no longer needed and after a few months I quit. My friend, on the other hand, continued. He excelled and is today an amazingly talented musician. I don't have any regrets in life, however, I wish I had kept taking lessons.

Great things take time to build. Not only time, but belief, courage, commitment and patience. Little steps everyday are powerful. Remember the drip that became the fast flowing river able to carve out canyons through the largest mountains? Great accomplishments are never achieved by excessive strength, but by persistence. Don't let fear hamper you. Stop thinking of all the work that is ahead of you. Do what it takes now, in this moment, just for today. Give it the best you've got. Stop concerning yourself with what happened in the past. Only look back to reflect on how far you've come. If I followed that advice, I would have been on stage with my own rock band years ago. Part of me still wants to be a rock star. I was the rabbit in the Tortoise and the Hare fable, forever waiting for the last minute to take any action. Nowadays, I'm more like a frog. The frog moves forward—unable to go backward. I'm not perfect, though, I do my best.

T.C. Hamlet's famous poem of two frogs in cream:

Two frogs were hopping side by side, not focusing on where they were going when suddenly they jumped into a bucket of fresh cream. Plop! They had to paddle to stay alive. It was too deep for them to stand up. One frog gave up after a few minutes and said, "What's the use? We're dead anyway," and it drowned. The other kept paddling with the hope that it could find a way out. An hour passed and the frog was tired. It kept paddling, only much slower. At the moment of exhaustion—there was nothing more it could do—it stopped paddling. It was then the frog felt a firm surface under its feet—butter. It had churned the cream with his webbed feet until it had made butter. When the happy frog had regained its breath, it jumped out of the bucket.

Which frog are you? The one that gives up easily? Or, the one that marches on no matter what? If we really want something then we'll find a way to get it. If not, we will find every excuse not to. Who cares if you screw up, it doesn't mean you're a failure. If I thought about how many times I have failed in my past, it would been enough for me to stop trying. We are not our past. Our past doesn't define us. Thomas Edison failed over one thousand times before he invented the light bulb. A dude named John Creasey got rejected seven hundred and fifty-three times before becoming a prolific English crime writer. He went on to write over five hundred and fifty books. The best leading scorers in sports have missed more times than they've scored.

How many times did you fall when you first learned to walk? Did you stop trying? Whatever you desire to do—just do it—no matter how scary it is. Your desire has to be greater than your fear. It all changes now...

## SHAKE IT UP
*"Throw your shoulders back and hold your head up high. Take a deep breath in and look up to the sky." Excerpt from the song 'I'm Gonna Fly' 1992 by Frank Di Genova*

Stagnant energy has to be dissipated before it can flow again. We need to break our limiting patterns and recharge our body. This doesn't mean we have to stick a metal fork in an electrical socket. We don't even have to put clamps from a car battery on our nipples. There are better ways. Oxygen contains a rich source of life force. We can literally energize our body just by breathing deeply. Try it now—take in a cavernous breath and hold it for a second or two. Now exhale, and yell out loud, "*Yes!*" Clap your hands and throw your fist in the air. Who cares if there are people around, they may need the entertainment. We need to do whatever it takes to get new energy moving. What can you think of?

Run on the spot, fist pump and yell, "Yeah baby!" Start dancing. You can't dance? Who cares. Sing your favourite song, or play it aloud. Go sing karaoke. Look around and see what you can be grateful for. Let's build the momentum. Yell loudly, "Today rocks, and I feel awesome!" Shake it, you're on fire baby!

Awaken your inner child, and buy a colouring book (they have adult ones now). Call your friends and have a guys/girls night out. Book a trip. Ride a bike. Be a kid again. Ask your friends for a game of hide and seek. Go for a run, do yoga, or hit a punching bag. If you're feeling adventurous go streaking... yes, you read that right. You could always go skinny dipping instead.

Sleep on the other side of the bed. Lay sideways or upside down. Sleep naked or with only one sock on. Pick up some weights and get your pump on. Go to a cooking class. Learn how to cook new exotic food. Do it naked, but watch for the hot oil. Get a new haircut and buy different clothes. Sign up for a pottery class. Go to a comedy show, but don't go naked.

If you've done any of these, you won't be feeling down. When we short circuit our old wiring, we create new possibilities. We open ourselves up to fresh ideas and new experiences. There is no way we can change our emotional state if we keep our head down and our shoulders slumped. The next time you feel sorry for yourself, stop... and shake it up!

Raise your vibration.

# CHAPTER TEN

# THE REBOOT

*"I think I've had enough of you, yes I really do. Stop standing in my way, get out, cuz I wanna live my life." Excerpt from the song 'Live My Life' 1987 by Frank Di Genova*

When our computer, smart phone or any device isn't working properly, a proven way to fix it is to shut it down and restart the system. In doing so, the operating network is reset and is able to function in the way it was intended. All the glitches are corrected, and the program runs smoothly again. Our body is no different. We are living machines that are prone to overload, and desensitization. Toxins from the environment, food, thoughts, and emotions can negatively affect our body and cause problems. Initially, these irritants don't pose much harm. However, over time the damage can be substantial, and can sometimes be irreversible. This chapter explains what these toxins are—and how to remove them, so we can live a healthy and vibrant life—mentally, emotionally and physically.

## COLD TURKEY

The only way I quit smoking two packs of cigarettes a day was to go cold turkey. I don't know how anyone can wean off them. I believe that an addiction is identified by the compulsive need for a substance or action. When this substance or action is removed/taken away we suffer withdrawal symptoms. In chapter five I discussed how our tolerance is built up as our receptors become desensitized, because we need more of the substance and get less stimulation in return. The first step in healing any addiction and to regain a normal tolerance level, is to reset our neurotransmitters. We do this by going cold turkey—not by weaning off. The subsequent steps involve removing the triggers and rewiring our neurological pathways. Success in this process is known when we have finally released our dependency.

## NOT SO FAST

Fasting is a protocol used to remove excess waste from the body. Our system naturally does a great job all on its own. However, the liver and other organs can only do so much. Help is needed to assist us with this process. Our body cannot purge itself of impurities if all of its energy is being used to deal with the garbage we keep ingesting. When we fast, food intake is partially or completely restricted—giving our system a chance to cleanse itself. This practice is observed all over the world and is found in many cultures—be it for religious or health reasons. We can apply this, not only to food, but to all harmful elements that can accumulate in the body.

Fasting is recorded as far back as seven thousand years, and is written in the ancient Veda scriptures of India. Animals are innately more in tune than humans are, when it comes to knowing what to do when they get sick. They find a safe place to hide, which is usually near a water source. All they do is rest, sleep and drink water. By doing so, they give their body a chance to heal and repair. Did you know that we fast every day? Well, not during the day, but at night when we sleep. It is during our sleep that we give our system time heal and regenerate. In the morning we break the fast. That's why it's called breakfast.

## RESISTANCE

What happens when you mix Charlie Sheen, cocaine and hookers together? You've got the perfect example of dopamine resistance. We're all suffering from some type of resistance, and we don't even know it. Before you think I'm accusing you of being a drug addict, hear me out. It doesn't have to be a substance—it could be mentally, emotionally or physically—it's all the same. Let me explain. Too many high glycemic foods can lead to insulin-resistance, and sometimes to serotonin-resistance. Being under artificial light when it's dark can keep our brain's serotonin levels elevated. This prevents the conversion to melatonin, which regulates our circadian rhythm—it's what makes us feel drowsy and gives us a goodnight sleep. They say everything in moderation, right? I beg to differ, as there are varying circumstances. Sure, eating a french fry or forgetting to floss your teeth is okay. But, a hit of heroin or an occasional drink for a recovering alcoholic isn't. I know people that can have one cigarette a day and not want any more. Personally,

I think they aren't human. The conveniences of modern life (technology) may cause some of us to feel off (whacked out.) These so called luxuries can cause neurotransmitter, hormone resistance and sensitivity. Avoidance is the best remedy, but how is that possible in our world today?

## THE CULPRITS

These fugitives aren't always associated with tobacco, marijuana, alcohol, pills and cocaine. There are many felons unbeknownst to us that could be stealing our vitality, and robbing us of our happiness. I was addicted to the worst criminal gang on the block—they were bad—sugar, salt, fatty foods, alcohol and caffeine. On their own they were awful enough, but together, they were venomous.

I was in toxic overload, mentally, emotionally, physically and environmentally. Stress was slowly killing me—my adrenals and nerves were shot. I was burnt out and suffered exhaustion. My clothes no longer fit, and I had to unbutton my pants whenever I sat. My thoughts were clouded, and I kept forgetting things. I was bloated, and worried that my farts would turn into a shitty mess. My crap was usually soft, and was responsible for what seemed like the never ending wipe. I should have invested in toilet paper stocks years ago!

Nothing motivated me. I had low energy. Sex wasn't enjoyable, and left me more tired than before. The daily grind of traffic, loud sirens, and car horns nearly drove me to the brink of insanity. I couldn't relax, my body was so tense. My back hurt and my temper was short. Climbing the stairs left me breathless—even tying my shoes was a struggle. I'd had enough. The time had come to do something about it.

This is where things are going to get a bit crazy, and I make no apologies. So, I suggest you go into your kitchen, grab some tinfoil, and make a hat—it will protect you. Not to worry, I'll wait for you—mine is already on.

Are you aware of other possible toxins assaulting your health? Have you heard of electromagnetic sensitivities? There is an increasing number of people who are developing sensitivities to electromagnetic fields, and radiation because we are swimming in a sea of electrical gunk produced by cell phones, computers, tv's, and bedside clock radios. Microwave ovens, fluorescent lights, wifi, bluetooth, satellite broadcasts and anything plugged in, all create harmful fields that compromise our health.

Do you live downtown and breathe in car exhaust fumes? Does your car have an air freshener hanging from the rear view mirror? Do you have plugin air fresheners in your home? Do you work with toxic chemicals? Does your home and workplace have adequate ventilation? Airborne pollutants are silent and invisible toxins. My salon was located on a busy downtown street. Daily, I'd breathe in colour, hairspray and perm fumes. Opening the door didn't help as stank city air and car exhaust fumes were waiting to enter.

Did you know that our skin absorbs everything we put on it? Would you eat your deodorant, toothpaste, makeup or facial cream? Would you drink your chemically made perfume, shampoo or conditioner? Personally, I would reconsider putting anything toxic on my skin—more so if I couldn't eat it. We can be exposed to over one hundred toxins per day. And that's not including all the chemicals that are in the processed food we eat. Our body is incredible. It can withstand a great deal of abuse, yet only for so long. How our body puts up with our abuse mystifies me.

Do you buy local meat, raised without antibodies and hormones? Do you eat organic vegetables that are grown in nutrient rich soil, and free of pesticides? Do you consume genetically modified foods? How would you know for sure? I didn't realize the food that I was eating contained harmful additives, preservatives, nitrates and artificial colouring. I do my best to avoid them.

How often do you clean your home? What types of cleaning agents do you use? Household cleaners are highly toxic—so are laundry detergent and fabric softeners. Is your hat still on? Do you drink your water straight from the tap? Or, from plastic bottles? Either way, you're ingesting fluoride, chlorine, BPA's and other toxic chemicals. When plastic is heated, carcinogenic compounds can leach out. Leaving water bottles exposed in the hot sun for long periods outside, or inside your car may not be the best idea. I was told that in production, bottled water is boiled before it's poured in the plastic containers. I've tried researching this and cannot verify it as fact. If true, it would mean that bottled water may not be the best choice—regardless if it's left in the sun or not.

Microwave ovens were banned in Russia in 1976 as studies proved negative consequences on people's health. The ban has since been lifted. When we use cling wrap, plastic or styrofoam containers in the microwave, we may be exposing ourselves to toxins. Microwaves may leach chemicals from these malleable containers. I'd stick with ceramic and glass bowls.

An accumulation of the aforementioned chemicals if used on a daily basis can calcify our pineal gland. What's the big deal? For starters, it makes us weak and lethargic. Our pineal gland is responsible for regulating our melatonin and circadian levels which affect our sleep-wake patterns. It is also referred to as the seat of our soul, or our third-eye. The question that often arises is, "What am I supposed to do, stop eating and drinking? I might as well be dead!" What can we do to reduce these toxins?

I'm not going to pick a fight with Big Pharma, or get into a debate between pro and anti vaccination. What I will say is, that it's a good idea to avoid popping pills like they were candy. I believe in medicine only when it's used to heal a condition, not to mask it. Excessive use of prescription drugs weakens the organs and immune system. Just because it's approved by the FDA doesn't mean it's good for us. The first time I saw a disclaimer on a drug commercial, I was in disbelief. Was this real or a joke? The listed side effects were longer than this whole chapter.

"Suffer from low testosterone? Take this product, feel like a man again. Side effects may include: cancer, dementia, suicidal tendencies, penis falling off—or death. If you experience any of these side effects please stop immediately." Those are encouraging odds, sign me up. Seriously though, are we so far removed from nature that we choose synthetic drugs over natural remedies? I am not preaching or telling you what to do, nor am I a doomsday guy. But doesn't it seem like cancer and other diseases are claiming our loved ones at an alarming rate? We can't live in a bubble, but we can make informed decisions about what we expose our bodies to.

## TAKING CONTROL

I avoid tap water as much as I can. Distilled water is devoid of minerals and may leach them from your body. The best form of water is natural spring water. Find a safe natural spring and collect the water in glass containers. You'll find natural springs closest to you, online. Make sure you test the water, and that it's not contaminated before you consume it. Our body benefits greatly from fresh air. If you're unable to get outdoors, investing in a reliable air purifier for the home is the next best solution.

Take an inventory of all the products that may be toxic in your home. Dump them, and choose natural products instead. Better yet, make your own. I do my best to make my own toothpaste and deodorant. I use coconut oil and baking powder. I don't wash my hair everyday like I used to, and I no longer use styling products. Coconut oil works well to keep my hair shinny. It feels healthier and is no longer dry and lifeless. My hair was once so dry and devoid of natural oils that it looked like I had pubic hair on my head! Now I wash it once a week, and in the winter add a small amount of coconut oil. In the summer I may wash it twice a week. I take a small dollop of coconut oil and put on my hands and massage it through, then rub my arms and face. Whatever is left over goes in my hair. I suggest adding a very small amount of oil to your hair, to avoid it looking greasy. You'll find plenty of personal hygiene and cleaning recipes and products, online. Here are some of my morning concoctions.

Homemade deodorant:

1/4 cup arrowroot flour

1/4 cup coconut oil

1/4 baking soda ( I use Bob Redmill)

*combine in a bowl until mixture is blended and place in small mason jars. Shower first and make sure armpits are dry. Use as desired, rub a small amount in hands first, then apply to underarms.


Toothpaste:

3 tbsp coconut oil

3 tbsp Bentonite clay power (use plastic or wooden spoon) the clay will absorb metal

1 tsp baking soda

1 small pinch of Himalayan salt or quality sea salt (adds minerals, disinfects)

1 pkt or less of stevia to add sweetness

5 drops of peppermint oil or any essential oils you prefer (clove, cinnamon, etc)

1 tsp calcium lactate

10 drops of trace minerals

Combine all ingredients in a glass, plastic or ceramic bowl (no metal) with a wooden or plastic spoon. Place it in a small glass jar with a tight fitting lid. Use a popsicle stick to avoid double dipping, and to avoid cross contamination. The toothpaste will last as long your coconut oils expiration date. If you want a basic toothpaste, use only coconut oil and baking soda. Personally, I like the clay's ability of removing toxins from my gums and mouth.

## RAISING YOUR VIBRATION PHYSICALLY

To raise our vibration we need to dissolve the dense energy that's lowering it. The *shake up* routines given in the last chapter are great ways to displace stagnant energy. We have to be a vibrational match to what we desire. If we are not oscillating in unison, there is no attraction—we are not in alignment. Remember the tuning forks in chapter seven?

Whatever we think, feel, speak and do, energy follows. This applies to the foods we eat, the music we listen to, and the people we hang out with. It works both ways—we are affected by what we are exposed to. What we watch and listen to greatly affects us, viewer discretion is advised. Pay attention to what your tv shows and movies imply—ditto for online social and news feeds, news and radio. Is it happy feel-good stuff? Are you seeing the picture? It doesn't end there.

How is your neighbourhood and work environment? Are your relationships happy or stressful? Everything is vibration. This doesn't mean that if you like jazz music and walk into a heavy metal concert that you'll turn into a headbanger. We may not notice at first—if at all—but after a while we become our environment. If you put a frog in boiling water, it will jump out. However, if you put it in cold water then slowly boil it, the frog will die without even being aware that the temperature is changing.

## FOOD

I could write a series of books on the topic of food, so I will keep this as short as possible. Food is complex, and is unlike alcohol, drugs or other substances, in that we need to eat it to survive. There's a fine line between necessity and addiction. Being Italian, I learned from a young age that food has many functions other than satiating hunger. An Italian mother shows her love by cooking and feeding her family. It's her role in the hierarchy—her identity. I'd often joke and impersonate a typical *mamma* and say, "Why you no eat, you sick? You no love me no more? You too skinny! You too fat! Why you get so fat? You should no eat too much! Why you eat too much?" I'm sure this is true for many other cultures.

I often ate out of hunger, but learned to eat for emotional nourishment. As result, I developed an unhealthy relationship with food. Eating was my *go to* when I didn't feel good. It was also a distraction for my boredom. I believe excess weight is condensed emotion—a protective layer. I was at my heaviest when I didn't feel good about myself. The stress hormone cortisol can pack on more pounds per day than calories ever can.

We celebrate birthdays, anniversaries, graduations and other festive observances by commemorating our accomplishments—with food. Cake, sweets and alcohol are the typical rewards. Recognition of obedient behaviour begins when we're babies in our highchair. We literally got high in our chair. Every time we're honoured with a treat, the sugar triggers an intense dopamine rush—and we became hooked. Reward with a dopamine rush is a dangerous mix. Food, like drinking, is cultural and social. Our eating patterns are learned behaviour. When we eat together around the family table we share stories and drink. Most often, we are so engaged that we don't even taste the food. Ask yourself, "Do I eat to live? Or, do I live to eat?

When we consume too much of the wrong types of food, our body gets thrown off balance. It becomes toxic, bloated and inflamed. This is how we get fat. Some people stay thin, yet still experience the adverse symptoms—which are fatigue, brain fog, aches, pains, digestive issues, allergies and headaches. Getting fat is not because one is weak or lazy, it's because their biology has been seized. Our tastebuds, brain chemistry, hormones and metabolism have been compromised. Did you know that sugar is eight times more addictive than cocaine? It hijacks the brain the same way. Excess salt, sugar and fat also seizes our body and brain's chemistry. These additives leave us helpless and addicted. No wonder junk food is the drug of choice. It would be easy to lose weight if it was just about calories in and calories out. Sugar calories are different.

Sugar triggers addiction and overeating. It spikes insulin levels and creates inflammation—which causes disease. Spiked insulin causes our body to store fat, and stops the sensation of being full so we're always craving more, and never feel satisfied. The result? We gain more weight. Consuming more than one teaspoon of sugar at a time (carbohydrates, alcohol and so on) spikes our blood sugar. The pancreas has to release insulin into our bloodstream to balance it. The excess is stored in our cells, and turns to fat. Have you ever felt a rush of energy right after you've drunk a soda-pop, or eaten a piece of cake? Have you noticed the crash not long after? It happens because our blood sugar gets too low. As a result, cortisol is produced and we crave more sugar.

When we get stressed, cortisol is released from the adrenal glands. It floods our blood with sugar, and causes a fight or flight response. Cortisol inhibits insulin production, so the sugar isn't stored, and is used by the muscles as fuel instead of our fat stores. As a result, our blood sugar drops and our brain tells us to eat more of it. That means more chips, more soda-pop, and more slices of pizza. Over time, constant cortisol release may lead to insulin resistance. Eventually our cells stop responding to insulin, and aren't able to absorb the glucose from our bloodstream. Our body cries for more insulin, but our pancreas isn't able to keep up. What do you think happens when we have all that sugar in our blood? Yes, it converts to fat. Long-term stress (cortisol induced) not only causes high blood sugar, but also adrenal fatigue and burnout. It may lead to type 2 diabetes. Sugar feeds our gut bacteria, and not in a good way. The result is an overgrowth of fungus and parasites. This leads to bloating, inflammation and an array of diseases.

A study was done by starving insulin resistant rats. They died without using any of their fat stores. The next time you feel like a bag chips, soda-pop or any type of stimulant, remember, you're at risk of opening Pandora's box. All it takes is one hit to trigger an addictive cycle. Just one blood sugar spike can unleash a sugar addiction. Not to mention hormonal and neurotransmitter resistance.

## THE RIGHT FOOD

In terms of vibration, raw fruits, vegetables, nuts, and seeds are the highest. Cooking them lowers their vibration, reduces their nutrients, and kills their life force. If your food source grows from the ground and is plant-based, you're eating right. Typically, the darker the skin, the more nutrients it has. There is a saying that has stuck with me for years. *Living food, living body—dead food, dead body.* Soaking nuts and seeds in water awakens, and activates their enzymes. They sprout to life, and supercharge our body. Try adding sprouted seeds and soaked nuts to your diet, and see how you feel.

According to the sages of India, beef and pork are the lowest vibrating of all the meats. Lamb is considered higher in vibration than other red meats, as is less taxing on our system. Some believe that all meat is bad. Others feel they can't do without it, and need it to stay healthy. Personally, I believe chicken and fish that are raised and euthanized in a respectful way is acceptable. If you must eat meat, the animal should be raised and fed organically without medication. It should be allowed to roam free in a large non-caged area. Eating a large salad with meat will help you to digest it better. Before an animal is slaughtered, I'm convinced that it's well aware of its impending death. The fear it experiences beforehand causes a release of a hormone into its body. When we eat their flesh we are energetically consuming their anxiety.

Non-fleshy foods also carry a lower vibration, and effect the body by lowering its energy. These include: processed, canned, packaged, genetically modified, fast food, fried, overcooked, burnt, and excess salt. They are toxic and filled with nitrates and other chemicals that we can't even pronounce. Try limiting eggs and dairy as much as possible, as they produce mucus and inflammation. If you have to get rid of any one thing, it would have to be *sugar*. It creates inflammation in our body, which causes disease.

Lower vibrating foods also create acidity in the body. An acid body is fertile for disease to develop. Disease can't thrive in an alkaline body. There are lists available online that indicate which foods are acid and alkaline forming. I have heard that lemons are the highest energetic food you can eat. They are great for alkalizing and cleansing an acidic body. Reduce or try to eliminate the evil whites: sugar, salt and white flour. When eating potatoes, don't peel the skin. When you do, you're left with starch—sugar! I suggest eating sweet potatoes (or yams) instead.

*In addition, saturated fats, trans-fats, and omega six oils (peanut, soy, corn, safflower, sunflower grape seed.) Also, refined carbohydrates, MSG, gluten, casein, aspartame, caffeine, alcohol, and smoking. Excessive coffee, black tea and stimulants play havoc on our nervous system—as do narcotics, pharmaceutical and recreational drugs.

I used to drink a lot of beer, wine and alcohol. These numb you down both emotionally and spiritually. In Ontario Canada, our alcohol is sold privately in stores called the LCBO. They use the subtitle and catch phrase, 'Wine-Spirits-Beer.' I drank them all, and they made me whine alright. It seems fitting that alcohol is called spirit. Have you noticed how it possesses and hampers one's common sense?

## LET ME IN

Are you addicted to porn? Each time we experience something that creates a rush within us, we become a bit more desensitized. It's similar to how our receptors and neurotransmitters react. We can only get our socks off for so long before our bodies adapt. Because we need more, we have to raise the bar higher the next time. This means kinkier sex, scarier horror movies, and weirder porn. The more violence, bad news, negative people, and stress we experience, the more numbed out we get—and the more normal it becomes. We acclimatize and our energy lowers. Remember, a vampire cannot enter your home unless he's invited first. It's time to push the reset button.

## MAKING SPACE

*Physical and non-physical decluttering*

Have you ever been stuck in traffic or in a large group of people and unable to move? Clutter restricts flow both physically and energetically, like dams in the river.

I just moved my father from his house, along with all the junk he no longer used—there was so much. Why do we collect things we don't use? When we simplify our life and release the things that no longer serve us, we create harmony and flow in out lives. Our junk is no different than our limiting thoughts and emotions. The bigger the purse the more junk that's stored. The bigger the house the more crap that's collected. It's not about having more space, it's about clearing it. Before we can receive fresh water in our pitcher, we need to empty out the old.

Here are a few suggestions you can do to declutter your home of stagnant energy: Clear your space and remove stuff you no longer use. Throw out stagnant items from your cupboards, closets, storage room and garage. Remove old spices from your kitchen, yes the ones on the back of the shelf that you forgot about. Chuck your skinny clothes or donate them.

By the time you fit back into them they'll be out of style. Let's get real, if you haven't needed anything in the last year or so, you never will. Sell them, or give them away to those who need it. The past is dead, it's no longer your identity. Neither are the experiences you hang onto which causes you pain and dis-ease. Besides being visually oppressive, they block the flow and prevent new energy from entering. The outside is a reflection of the inside.

Declutter the stories you keep playing in your head. Remove negative thoughts and obsessive thinking. Discard your need for approval and victim identity. Toss out negative friends and beliefs. Stop watching horror, violent and pornographic movies. Drop the excuses, the drugs and alcohol—stay away from their triggers. Let go of the past. Set new goals and intents. Simplify your life. If it's toxic, dump it.

Pay attention to your thoughts and use empowering words. Embrace the emotions that arise, with gratitude, let them go. The ripples of restless thoughts distort the image of the moon reflected in the puddle of water. When you can still your mind, you will see your true essence in the stillness.

## CALL OF NATURE

*I wish I had listened to my father when he told me to, "Go jump in the lake."*

Have you ever heard of earthing, or grounding as some people refer to it? Earthing is similar to grounding your energy after a meditation or healing session. Before we started wearing rubber soled shoes we naturally connected to the Earth. The Earth is abundant with negatively charged free-electrons.

They're available to us when we connect with her directly. Some of you already know that free radicals are created in our system when we smoke, ingest pollutants, and exercise excessively. Negative ions are known for being a great antioxidant to remove these toxins. We are bombarded with electro-magnetic radiation from computers, mobile phones, radio, tv's, wifi, and anything that's plugged in. These fields disrupt the subtle energetic communications in our body.

The easiest way to ground is to walk barefoot on grass or soil—anything in nature will conduct. If you're hardcore, get naked and bury yourself in a hole for twenty minutes. If that's too much, you can, "Go jump in the lake." More skin—more surface—more contact. Maybe Pagans were onto something when they touched wood for good luck. This is where the saying, *knock on wood* comes from. They believed that benevolent spirits dwelled in the trees. Some consider they are the trees themselves. Are you a tree hugger? Now you know why.

There are more people swearing by this method of pain management and overall well-being. The only way to know for sure is to try it for yourself. Decreased inflammation, less stress, better sleep and an array of other benefits have been known to occur by earth-grounding. Take off your shoes and socks, and give it a go. If you can't get outside you can buy grounding mats, bed sheets and other products. They are available online and in some specialty stores.

## UNPLUGGED

The music industry has coined a term for artists when they play an acoustic version of their non-acoustic songs. They call it unplugged. The songs are performed and recorded without any electronic instruments. This changes the expression and emotion of the music. Living our lives unplugged is the best way to restore our health and vitality. In modern society this is difficult to do, unless we live far away from the city. One way around this is to detox and reset on all levels.

Spend as much time as you can in nature. Go camping, or rent a cottage (preferably by water) for a week or two. Shut off your cell phone, clock radio, computer and all technology. This includes tv and radio. Try going completely powerless. Did you know that you can regulate your serotonin and melatonin levels simply by going without artificial light for a month? You may love the city and all its amenities, but what you don't know is how it's slowly destroying your health and creating disease. It will do you good to get away from the rat race, the noise, and the sea of electro and physical pollution. Even if it's only for a few days or a week, you'll feel the difference. Another option is to go online and find an electromagnetic-free retreat. There, they take care of everything for you. Alternatively, sign up for a Vipassana meditation retreat, where you're in complete silence for ten days. You can't talk, read, journal, or listen to music—absolutely no distractions.

Unplugging from anything isn't easy. I won't sugarcoat it. Going through any kind of withdrawal can at times feel like hell. When shit starts getting real, we have nothing to distract ourselves. We are without our escape mechanisms, and left to face the demons that we've been avoiding. Most of us are unwilling to meet our pain, and choose instead to use painkillers—in whatever form.

## PROTOCOLS

The following are hard reboots to reset our receptors and neurotransmitters. They are methods to cleanse and detox our system.

## THE BREATH

In Eastern teachings, it's believed our lifespan is measured in the number of breaths we take. A Giant Tortoise breathes only four times a minute and can live up to one-hundred and fifty years. Monkeys breathe thirty-two times a minute and have a significantly lower lifespan—around eighteen years. Mice live only one to two years, and breathe over one-hundred and fifty times a minute. This is not to say that if we hold our breath we will live longer. It doesn't matter if we hold it consciously, or due to feeling fear. Doing so puts stress on the heart. If we are stressed, our tendency is to breathe quick and shallow. This causes us to hyperventilate and go into a fight or flight mode. We lose our awareness of being mindful and our ability to feel beyond our fear. Stress compromises our health, and so does improper breathing.

Meditation is a great way to slow and regulate the breath, and to become aware of where your breath is coming from. Is it from high in your chest, or deep in your diaphragm? Is it fast, slow, shallow or deep? Breathing not only removes waste via carbon dioxide, it also helps relieve tension, physical, and emotional pain. Eating alkalizing type foods isn't the only way to keep the body from becoming too acidic. Deep breathing is just as effective, if not, more so.

Take three slow deep breaths, hold them slightly on the inhale and exhale. Do this a few times a day and as part of your morning routine. Your body and brain will thank you.

WATER FAST:
Duration is 24 to 72 hours
What you will need:
Water, preferably natural spring.

This is hardcore, yet, it only takes twenty-four hours to reset the body. This is like shutting down your computer or smart phone. This is done to release your body's craving for sugar, salt and fat. It's not for the faint of heart. Some consider this easier than the nine day juice cleanse (to follow). Personally, I rather the slower method of a juice fast, which is less extreme. A water fast only resets your receptors and doesn't effectively rid the body of toxins. Plan a day off and have someone with you. You may not want to get out of bed. Consult with your doctor before you attempt this.

Your first water fast should only be twenty-four hours. Then, if you feel like you want to attempt a longer one, increase your days incrementally. Some people have been known to do thirty days. This wouldn't be my first choice. I feel three days is enough to fully reset. Take those days off and prepare to do nothing. Side effects can include headaches, dizziness and nausea. It usually hits you late in the afternoon. Get as much rest as you can.

This fast is not only to reset your system, you will also meet yourself, your ego and your pain. I consider this a psychological introduction to your dark side. Just ride it out.

Drink approximately ten 8 oz. glasses each day. Spread them out, don't drink them all at once. Break your fast the next day with juice, fruit, then cooked veggies. Keep your workload low, and don't exercise during the fast.

*There is a misconception that the more water you drink the better. This isn't true, too much water isn't good.

JUICE CLEANSE:
Duration is 7 to 9 days
What you will need:
Juice from citrus fruits and vegetables. You will also need small mason jars with non-leak lids, thermal lunch bag, and one to two cryogenic ice packs. If possible, buy organic produce. For the next seven to nine days you will drink only juice. I'm not talking about packaged juice which has been pasteurized. This juice is basically sugar and is devoid of its living enzymes. You can buy a high quality juicer and make your own, or, buy it fresh from juice bars. Many businesses now offer detox packages that can be delivered or picked up daily. They prepare everything for you, so it's easy. Since we want to remove sugar, juice veggies in preference to fruits. Lemons and grapefruits are acceptable. We also want to detox from salt, fat, caffeine and alcohol, so avoid these. Drink a glass of juice every couple of hours or so.

This is much easier than the water fast and is considered a partial fast. If you need the sensation of eating, have a large raw salad made with organic romaine lettuce. Add fresh lemon juice and a pinch of high quality sea salt. My personal preference is Himalayan salt. It's actually better for you because it contains 84 trace minerals that are found in the human body. Make a batch of juice to last you for two days. After three days the enzymes start to oxidize and deteriorate. Fill small mason jars and seal with leakproof lids. Refrigerate immediately after juicing. Place jars into a thermal lunch bag and put in a cryogenic ice pack. Pack as many jars as you need for the day.

My Sample:
5 celery stalks
1 cucumber
1 bunch parsley and/or cilantro
1 inch ginger and turmeric roots
2 apples (sliced)
1 lemon (peeled if not organic)
1 raw habanero pepper (adjust for tolerance)

This won't make much so you'll have to increase the amount. I've given you the proportions between these ingredients. There are no rules, you can add or remove what you want. I like apples in my juice, they give me a bit of energy and add sweetness. They should be omitted, but I convince myself that they contain natural sugar and it's okay. You can add carrot, beet or whatever you like. I try not to use high glycemic root vegetables when I cleanse.

When your fast is complete, introduce heavier food slowly so you don't shock your system. Also, pay attention to how your body feels when you do. This is a good opportunity to see what your body likes and what it doesn't. You can revise a diet that works best for you. I recommend www.rebootwithjoe.com, it is an excellent site and has everything you need to know about juicing.

## WHAT YOU CAN EXPECT

I share my experiences so they may help you to navigate through yours. Everyone's body is different and each may react in varying ways.

The first three to four days are the toughest. However, it gets easier as each day passes. I used to drink a lot of coffee so I endured massive headaches—my body wasn't happy without its caffeine. My energy plummeted and I felt dizzy. I couldn't focus and kept forgetting things. My body was in pain, especially my lower back. I was irritable and had major mood swings. Sometimes, I felt like I was dying. Although that was most likely my ego. It was almost enough to force me to give up. "*Why am I doing this?*" I thought. *This is bullshit, I'd rather feel how I did before this cleanse!*" I fought that mental war many times an hour and was often at the brink of giving up. I thought of every excuse I could to stop. The problem was, I was fighting against years of ingrained habits and subconscious programming which sought to keep me in my comfort zone. I wasn't going to give in, or take the easy way out. After the fourth day it was almost smooth sailing.

Breaking our conditioning is an arduous task, and takes diligence and courage to persevere. A profound healing takes place when you carry your cross, and it's only realized after you do. There is a difference between suffering as the victim versus enduring a right of passage. Perhaps the false premise of *no pain no gain* comes from this notion.

## SMOOTHIE DIET

Duration: 1 week only (use as a meal replacement or a fasting protocol)

What you will need:

High powered blender, spring water, and ingredients. The sky is the limit regarding ingredients, there are many combinations. For the base (liquid) you can use coconut or spring water, almond or soy milk. From there you can add your fruits and vegetables. Add frozen berries, bananas, avocados, and so on. You can grab a ton of recipes online.

My sample breakfast:

2 bananas (frozen)

2 cups coconut water (fresh if possible)

1 bunch raw spinach

There is a debate on which is better, juicing versus blending. Each is different and both have benefits. Juice permeates the cells and stomach lining faster than smoothies do. Smoothies keep you feeling fuller longer, as the nutrients are absorbed slower. The difference is like burning kindling compared to a log. I suggest you do both to maximize the benifits of each.

When you're not juice fasting I recommend you observe partial fasting, to keep your body working optimally. My suggestion is to only drink juice one day per week or three consecutive days each month. Also try intermittent fasting. This means restricting your eating to a shorter time span. Instead of a ten to twelve hour interval between dinner and breakfast (this includes a late night snack), try a twelve to fourteen hour window—or more. Skip meals every so often to give your system a break. The yogis of India say, "If you want to live longer, eat less."

Visit my website for more information on fasting and detailed protocols. Download free programs at www.frankdigenova. com

# CHAPTER ELEVEN

# RELEASING

*"I surrender everything, all my joy and all my pain inside.
I surrender everything until there's no place left to hide."
Excerpt from the song 'I Surrender' 1998 by Frank Di Genova*

Gratitude is one of the best ways to raise our vibration. Complaining lowers it. When we're grateful we are open to receive more. It acknowledges our worth, and shows respect to oneself. Saying, "I am grateful" has a higher vibration than saying, "Thank you." The latter has been overused and has lost its true meaning—so have the words *I'm sorry* and *I promise*.

## GRATITUDE

Being thankful is appreciating what we have on our plate (figurativley speaking). It is knowing that we have more than enough. Those that are selfish and ungrateful, typically look at the platter and feel that they didn't get enough. Resentment happens when we feel bitter for being treated unfairly—it can reinforce our sense of lack and feelings of being undeserving.

The nature of the mind/ego equate to a person's worth, is governed by the things they have or own. Conversely, when we don't *have* these things, we lack self-worth.

How can life give us more if we're not grateful for what we have now? Do you know that most of our daily thoughts can be negative? These thoughts are usually the same ones that repeat, day after day. Gratitude redirects our mind to think and feel thoughts in a more positive way, and raises our vibration. Have you noticed that when you have a good day, you don't give it a second thought? But, when your day is less than stellar and something goes awry, it's all we talk about. The secret, is to be grateful for whatever arises—regardless of whether we think it's good, or bad. Make it a practice to appreciate what you have. Don't let an unfortunate event be what makes you realize what you had and didn't appreciate. Be grateful for everyone and everything in your life. Your health, your family, and your friends. Be thankful for whatever is in your pocket, even if it's just a tissue.

What might we be grateful for? Do you feel there is no good in your life? Before you throw your next pity party consider this: If you haven't fought in a war, been in prison or tortured, you are not part of the half billion people who have been. If you can talk freely about your religious beliefs and go to church without being harassed or tortured, there are three billion people who can't. Do you have food in your fridge, clothes in your closet, a bed to sleep in, and a roof over your head? Congratulations, you're richer than seventy-five percent of the people in the world. If you have extra money that you can donate, and are able to buy things you want, you're in the top eight percent of the wealthiest in the world. The fact that you can read these words means that you're more fortunate than two billion people who can't. Do you still feel like you have nothing? Are you still suffering because of it? I'm asking only to show you contrast, not to make you feel guilty.

When you wake up tomorrow morning, take a few deep breaths. Be thankful you're alive and can breathe. Be thankful for everything you have: from the warm water that magically comes out of the pipes, to being stuck in traffic because you can afford a car. When next using the toilet, be thankful. It's not just pee and pooh being released but the by-product of what has hydrated and nourished you. Be even more thankful for the toilet paper.

## GOODNIGHT/GOOD MORNING

The two most crucial times that our mind is easily impressed upon, is just before we fall asleep, and as soon as we wake. When sleep comes, our thoughts and consciousness drift—all resistance dissolves. Whatever was last seen, felt or heard is impressed upon our subconscious. This is why it's a good idea to remove tv's, tablets, and smartphones from your bedroom—even your clock radio. I must confess, sometimes I'll indulge in late night radio. The last thing we need to take to bed is fear-based media. How many of you wake up to a loud pulsating alarm? I feel that it would be a traumatic way to start your day. If you enjoy reading before bed, try an inspirational book. Or, enjoy some quiet time. Take a warm bath or shower. I find meditating for twenty minutes before bed helps the mind settle.

The moment we wake, our mind is a clear canvas—a dry sponge ready to absorb new thoughts. We have eighty-six thousand-four-hundred seconds each day that are available to us. How will you invest in them? Every second is valuable. What will you pay attention to? Yesterday doesn't exist anymore. Drop it, there's no need to hang on to it. Negative thoughts from the past are like thieves that creep into the present to steal our happiness. Your subconscious has a security system. Enable it. Only allow positive thoughts and feelings to enter.

## GRATITUDE JOURNAL

You'll need a notebook—blank or lined. Choose your favourite pen or writing tool of choice. On the cover write, 'Things That I Am Grateful For.' Place it by your bedside table. Make sure you can see it. I used to keep mine in the drawer and would always forget about it. Out of sight, out of mind.

Every morning write down three things that you're grateful for. Make sure they are different each day. They can be about anything: your body, what you have accomplished, or the people in your life, and so on. Read them aloud before you start your day.

Each night before going to bed, write underneath your morning's entry, three things that went right that day. Explain how and why they did. Re-read your morning's gratitude along with your new entry before you fall asleep. Do this for a minimum of thirty days, and watch your life magically change. Mine did after only seven days. Aim for a daily practice. Sometimes you'll forget to make an entry or won't be able to. You may be staying overnight with friends or family. Whatever the case, don't be hard on yourself. Take the notebook with you, or make post-it notes and read them throughout the day. You are building a new habit, so don't worry if you forget sometimes. Another tool to explore is to write a list of intentions, or create a vision board. There are many references available online.

## MONKEY NUTS

In India they catch monkeys by making a hole in a box just big enough for it to put it's hand through. Nuts are placed inside the box within the monkeys reach. When it senses the bait it puts its hand through the opening and grabs the nuts, making a fist. The hand holding the nuts is too big to slide back out through the hole. You would think the primate would figure it out and just let go. Simple right? What are we holding on to that's trapping us? What things do we need to surrender, accept and forgive, to free ourselves from their grip?

## SURRENDER, ACCEPT, FORGIVE

Surrendering doesn't mean we've lost, or that we have thrown in the towel. We're letting go of our need to control, our need for approval, and our need to struggle. Yielding means being authentic, transparent, and not hiding anymore. Letting go doesn't mean giving away our stuff against our will. It means releasing our attachment to it. We tend to hang onto things to feel secure, and give us a sense of identity. When we can let go we are able to acknowledge that we don't need it, and it is no longer a condition required for our happiness. If we can't let go, then it has us—we don't have it. When we create space, we can receive more.

Acceptance is allowing, and being okay with whatever is happening. We observe this without judgement or resistance. Accepting a situation is not needing to change or control what's arising. Whatever comes up, accept it, it's a gift. Have you ever thought that we may be responsible for what emerges in our lives?

To forgive another is not a sign of weakness. It's not a way to let others off the hook. Forgiveness is a higher form of love, it's seeing ourselves in others. Absolving all who trespass against us frees us from them and our past. It allows us to receive openly without judgment. No one is perfect, we all screw up. Whether something is done against us, in spite or not—it doesn't matter. It all comes from pain, which must be healed, not perpetuated. Do you believe that if you, or another knew a better way to respond, they would? We're all doing the best we can with the knowledge we have. Compassion heals.

When we forgive another, we are actually forgiving ourselves. We are each others mirrors. There are many techniques available on forgiveness, however, the one I like is the Ho'oponopono prayer. This technique is an ancient Hawaiian practice, and it means *to make right* thru reconciliation and forgiveness. We've all perceived being treated unfairly at some point in our lives—the reasons vary. A person may not like you, and not know why—they just do. Mostly, it's a karmic debt, and ancestral. It may be from something that happened yesterday, or from an old feud that occurred many lifetimes ago. There is a tendency to build a case around who is right, and who isn't. It doesn't matter, the point is moot. What matters is that we heal these wounds.

From a place of love and compassion we can forgive others and ourselves by silently expressing the following phrase. The person need not be present. Visualizing the person you want to forgive and repeat the Ho'oponopono prayer:

I love you... I'm sorry... Please forgive me... Thank you.

I love you... I'm sorry... Please forgive me... Thank you

I love you... I'm sorry... Please forgive me... Thank you

I love you... I'm sorry... Please forgive me... Thank you

## THE INNER VOICE & CHANGING BELIEFS

Our thoughts or inner voice are whispers to the universe. Words are the manifested expression of these thoughts—they become our outside voice. We live in a vibrational world, so it doesn't matter whether we say them aloud or not. Emotions work the same.

Whenever we vibrate, *I can't, I'll try, I should, I need, I have to*—we're limiting and disempowering ourselves. Replace them with, *I can, I will, and I choose*—notice how better they feel. Unless you're high on angel-dust or LSD, saying *"I can fly"* doesn't mean you can. Over time, these positive affirmations slowly reprogram our subconscious mind, and raise our energy.

Every time we self-deprecate, even as a joke, we're lowering our energy. By doing so we attract like energies. Our subconscious doesn't have a sense of humour, it just follows commands. Saying, *"Fuck my life, just my luck, this always happens to me, I never win anything, figures, I'm so stupid,"* are commands that imprint into our psyche. So are, *"I am lucky, awesome things always happen to me, I am learning new stuff everyday... I am grateful."*

A powerful way to bypass our conscious mind and plug straight into our subconscious, is by using the words, "I AM." There is no maybe, no doubt, and it isn't up for discussion—it just is. These words are simple, powerful and absolute. Whatever we declare after them, manifests. Repeat every morning and see how you feel: "I AM abundant, I AM healthy, I AM grateful, I AM Love."

Mizaru, Kikazaru, Iwazaru, are the famous 'Three Monkeys,' *that see no evil, hear no evil, and speak no evil.'* They're depicted as covering their eyes, mouth and ears. A camera will only capture what's in its visual field. Interesting, that the photographer holding the camera cannot see themselves in the frame. What does this mean? It means that we are the observer. What are we observing? We only see what we pay attention to. It doesn't matter how we see, but what we see. If you don't want it in your experience, don't bring it in—it's that simple.

Most people complain about what they don't want. Yet, are surprised when that's all they get. Are you following me? Let me explain. Think of a red ball, but don't think of a pink elephant. Were you successful? Or, did you think of both? Even if you don't want to focus on something, you still do. There is truth to the saying, *out of sight out of mind.* This is only true as long as we're not resisting or pushing it away—denial.

## DEEP SURRENDER

We don't get sick or diseased overnight. It takes time for energy to condense, and manifest from thought to emotion, and into the physical. Negative thought patterns which are held on to, are responsible for our pain and disease. When we let them go, they dissipate. Whenever there is pain present, there is resistance in some form. It doesn't matter if it's physical or emotional, it's still pain. Many have the belief that suffering happens to us, and think that something outside ourselves is responsible. When in fact, it's our creation. This runs counter-intuitive to rational thinking. Why would we want to self-inflict pain, or intentionally harm ourselves? Could it be because of our low self-worth? Our desire to punish ourselves? Do we think we deserve it?

Consciously, we can't accept this fact so we blame another—but really, we blame ourself. Whatever the case, there are various coping mechanisms—suppressing, burying and numbing to name a few. We think if we allow a situation to surface, it may get worse, or that it may happen again. We become entrusted gatekeepers hiding and protecting our pain. Or, we transform into great storytellers that perpetuate an identity of being a victim. Instead of carrying the badge of the martyr, or the vengeance of a vigilante... surrender.

You're good enough for great things to happen, and when they do, there is no need to sabotage it.

## ENERGY BODY BATH

This exercise can be done whenever you feel tension or resistance in any part of your body. It's a great way to relax anytime you feel stressed, and is a natural alternative to pain management. I suggest doing the *Leaf It Alone* meditation before doing any exercise in this chapter. It will help put you in a more receptive state and lessen your resistance.

This unique process draws energy into an area, and displaces the stagnate energy. It reduces pain, tension and circulates new energy. It will leave you feeling refreshed and energized. Make sure you drink plenty of water after doing any releasing protocols, as it assists in flushing toxins from the body.

You can sit in a chair or lie down (recommended). Find a comfortable position where you can relax deeply, and not be disturbed. When you're ready, and with your eyes closed, focus on your left foot. Begin breathing deeply and slowly. After a few breaths completely tense your foot—contract all its muscles—curl in your toes. Hold the tension for three full breaths, as you inhale and exhale deeply. On the last exhale, release all the tension slowly. Imagine it deflating like a balloon. Continue releasing with a few more breaths. Feel the tension wash away and relax. Imagine that your foot has turned to stone.

Move on to your right foot and do the same. Keep your left foot as relaxed as possible. Continue with your left calf and thigh, then to your right calf and thigh. If you find this difficult at first, you can contract your whole foot and leg at once. As you progress in this practice, you will find it easier to isolate each body part. The intent here is to take your time and not rush through this process. Move on to your hips, then to your buttocks, genital area, torso, lower back and abdominal area. Tense each part in succession, hold and release them like in the example of your left foot. Make a fist with your left hand and contract your arm. Then after you've done the same with your right, proceed to your shoulders and neck.

*We always start with the left side first, as this side is the feminine. It is like opening the door for a woman. The left side also represents *yin*, while the right is *yang*. Energy moves from negative to positive. When you receive money, use your left hand. When you release it, use your right hand.

Lastly, tense your face, press you lips together and squeeze your eyes. When you have completed tensing and relaxing your whole body, feel into the peace and calm. You want to enjoy this, so stay with it. What use would it be if you got up quickly? It would be like filling up a bucket of water drop by drop, then kicking it over. The purpose here is to integrate and absorb the calmness you've brought into your being.

*\*You may experience heaviness, lightness or buzzing energy around your body afterward. This is normal. If you have an injury in a specific part of your body, be gentle when you tense that area. Be sure to breathe into and focus your attention on the area you want the energy to go. Imagine that the intended body part is breathing healing energy into itself. Visualize a mouth or a nose if it helps. If the area is stiff, imagine warm energy flowing to it. For inflamed areas, breathe in cool soothing energy. Lightly tense and release these areas while you visualize the warm and cool sensations. You have your own energetic heat and ice packs. Inhaling while tensing, draws in energy. Exhaling circulates and releases energy. Doing this helps the energy to flow, so does vigorous rubbing of the area on the skin.*

## SPICY CHOCOLATE

Self-healing isn't something we jump into, because we know it isn't the same as eating a piece of cake. There's no sugarcoating the process, shit can get very real. If you have ever eaten spicy chocolate you know the contrast that I'm talking about. The chocolate is sweet, but not enough to fully douse the heat, and just enough to take the edge off. It is the same with releasing discomfort and traumatic events. This exercise will allow you to taste the realization of what you've been avoiding, and to finally release it.

What we ignore escalates, until we pay attention to it. It's like a child vying for their parents attention. Have you noticed how they do that when their parent is busy talking to another? Pain just wants to say, "Listen to me, there is something I need to tell you." So, meet it, let it arise. By doing so we give it a personal audience, and it will release. There comes a time when painkillers and our ways of avoidance stop working. Instead, they start to slowly kill us. We can't change the past, but we can release it.

## LET'S TAKE A BITE

This exercise is best done after the Energy Body Bath. You could also do this in bed, as you're comfortably lying down. Ask your higher self what is needing to be shown at this time. Literally ask yourself, "What am I holding back that wants to express itself?" If you're already aware of what it is, let it arise. The first step is to get in touch with your breath, to relax, and detach from your thoughts—feel your body. Scan every body part with your full awareness, breathing deeply into each area. Do you notice any tension? Continue to breathe slowly and deeply, maintaining your focus throughout the process. Often there is a tendency for our breathing to become shallow. Some subconsciously hold their breath during the spicy moments—breathe through it.

Allow any discomfort to be present. We're not trying to get rid of anything. We're only wanting to let it express itself. Feel it... without resistance... all of it. If the mind scurries away, bring your attention back to its core. Where are you experiencing it in your body? Breathe... observe its shape, colour, and texture. What else do you notice about it? Breathe into it... is it big or small, does it feel sharp or dull? Breathe... does it move around or stay in one spot? Breathe... allow the discomfort to fully express itself... release all tension.

Breathe... are there any thoughts, memories or emotions that are surfacing? How do you feel? Let them bubble up. Remember, do not identify with them—you're only watching them unfold as an experience. Whatever arises doesn't belong to you. Breathe... there is no judgement... breathe. Allow without resistance... if there is, where do you feel it? Breathe... what thoughts and emotions are revealing themselves? Are they positive, negative, or indifferent?

If your awareness shifts, bring it back. Breathe... remember it's your experience, not your identity. It doesn't belong to you, it doesn't define you... it's not your responsibility. Don't engage... be the witness. What stories have you been telling around what is arising? What do you believe to be true about it? Release... let it all go.

Breathe... fully love what is arising—have compassion for self. Be grateful, embrace it. Thank it for showing up. Forgive yourself for ignoring it. Rejoice, it's finally being heard. As the reality collapses, the stagnant and dense energy will start to dissolve. Love yourself. You are perfect just as you are. Breathe... you are releasing your past.

## EMOTIONAL ORGAN RELEASE

This exercise is best done after the Energy Body Bath. You could also do this in bed, as you're comfortably lying down. Releasing stagnant energy from our organs is an important part of self-healing. Most of us neglect our body and organs. We often abuse them with food, stimulants and negative thinking. This is a great exercise for healing and appreciating your organs. They'll love the attention. If it helps, you can place your hands on the area you're focusing on.

Start by focusing on the kidneys. They are located on either side of the body, underneath the diaphragm near the lower back. They hold the vibration of fear and are weakened by it. Breathe into your kidneys and send them all your love. Say, "I'm sorry for not treating you well, please forgive me." Be mindful to breathe deeply throughout this process. Thank them for filtering your blood of excess salt, toxins, and waste. Tell your kidneys they are loved and appreciated. Hold this intent for a few minutes, and when you're ready, move on to the spleen.

Focus on the spleen. It is located under the ribcage and above the stomach in the left upper quadrant of the abdomen. The spleen holds on to our pensiveness and worry. Breathe into it and say, "I'm sorry for mistreating you with my anxiety and overthinking." When we forgive, we are forgiven. There is no rejection because there is no separation. Thank your spleen for keeping your immune system strong, and for removing viruses and toxins from your body. Send it love and appreciation. Hold this intent for a few minutes, and when you're ready, move on to the liver.

Next, focus on your liver. It is located in the right upper part of the abdomen, beneath the diaphragm and is protected by the lower right ribs. The liver holds on to our anger. Breathe deeply, and send it love and compassion. Apologize for mistreating it with your anger, excessive alcohol or whatever it has had to deal with. Forgive your liver and yourself for all you've done to it. Thank it for detoxifying your blood, and for producing bile. Since you're in close proximity to your gallbladder you may like to repeat this process. It is located directly beneath your liver. Thank it for hanging on to the bile and unexpressed anger. Flood it with love by placing your hands over the area in appreciation. If you have had your gallbladder removed, its energetic blue print is still there—you can still address it. Hold this intent for a few minutes, and when you're ready, move on to the lungs.

The lungs are located on either side of the chest. Tell them you're sorry for taxing them with your suffering. Tell them it's safe to fully breathe in life. Apologize for abusing them by smoking and inhaling toxic fumes. Forgive yourself... they'll be happy. Thank them for giving you fresh oxygen and for removing carbon dioxide from your body. Hold this intent for a few minutes, and when you're ready, move on to the heart.

Imagine an emerald green light encompassing your heart. It is located in the chest between the lungs and behind the sternum just above the diaphragm—slightly to the left side of the body. Visualize this light saturating your heart with complete joy. Apologize for not loving yourself unconditionally and for pushing love away. Forgive your heart for all the times you've rejected love, approval and self-worth. Thank it for keeping you alive and for pumping blood throughout your body. "Dear heart, you are loved, appreciated and accepted one-hundred percent. I love you." Hold this intent for a few minutes, and when you're ready, send love to your whole body.

Continue thanking your eyes for giving you sight, your ears for allowing you to hear and so forth. Grab an anatomy book and study other body parts and locations. Visualize, and send each area your love and compassion. You can also research what herbs are good for cleansing your organs. Chinese medicine uses herbal elixirs and various mind/body practices. I highly recommend it.

## EMOTIONAL CHAKRA CLEANSE

There are seven energy centres located along the spine, they are called Chakra's. Energy flows through them when they're open, and is blocked when they're closed. Our health and vitality are affected by unbalanced Chakras.

The Root Chakra is located at the base of spine in the tailbone area. It's our survival centre, and is blocked by *Fear*. (Represents the element of earth)

The Sacral Chakra is located in the lower abdomen, about two inches below the navel. It represents pleasure, sexuality and creativity, and is blocked by *Guilt*. (Represents the element of water)

The Solar Plexus Chakra is located in the upper abdomen below the rib cage and diaphragm. It represents willpower, self-worth and confidence, and is blocked by *Shame*. (Represents the element of fire)

The Heart Chakra is located in the centre of the chest. It represents love and our ability to feel and express compassion, empathy, humility, and is blocked by *Grief.* (Represents the element of air)

The Throat Chakra is located at the centre of the neck and shoulders. It represents communication and our self-expression. It symbolizes our truth, and is blocked by *Lies* (deceit). (Represents sound)

The Third Eye Charka is located at the forehead between the eyebrows. It represents Insight (clarity and vision). This is our psychic centre and our (intuition) inner and outer world symbolic language, and is blocked by *Illusion.* (Represents light)

The Crown Chakra is located at the top of the head. It represents our awareness and thoughts, and is our connection with our Highest Self (Source.) This Chakra is blocked by our worldly *Attachments.* (Represents thought)

BEGIN:

Spend a few minutes on each area, and allow whatever needs to arise. Allow it to dissolve.

Place your attention on your Root Chakra. Breathe in red healing energy from the Earth. Let go of all fear-based feelings that arise... surrender. You are safe. It's okay, it's not real. Breathe it away.

Place your attention on your Sacral Chakra. Imagine wading through the ocean as its waves wash away your guilt. Visualize orange rays from a deep sunset disintegrating any that you've stored. What do you blame yourself for? Forgive yourself, you did the best you could. Release... breathe. It's not your fault.

Place your attention on your Solar Plexus Chakra. Breathe in healing yellow light from the midday sun. What are the things that have disappointed you in your life? Accept every aspect, including your mistakes. We all make them—we are imperfectly perfect. Embrace all that you are. You are powerful.

Place your attention on your Heart Chakra. Breathe in healing green energy from the trees and from all of Mother Earth's vegetation. Feel and let go of all your sadness and grief. Breathe in love and compassion. You are love, and are loved. Visualize a green flower blossoming from your heart.

Place your attention on your Throat Chakra. Breathe in blue energy coming from the sky. Let go of all the lies you've told yourself and others. Release all the things you've denied. Breathe in your truth. You are free and safe to express yourself. You are heard.

Place your attention on the space between your eyebrows at your forehead (Third eye). Breathe in a healing indigo light. Release all judgments about yourself and others, and the illusion that we're all separate. We're living on this planet together. We are One, all connected.

Place your attention at the very top of your head (Crown Chakra). Breathe in a violet light coming in from your higher self. Let it come from the centre of our galaxy, streaming into your head and throughout your entire body. Release all earthly attachments. Notice what you're holding on to, and what attracts you to this world. Let it go. We are children of the universe.

## THE ULTIMATE SELFIE

The ultimate selfie isn't accomplished with a camera, it's done by using a mirror. Go ahead. See your reflection in a mirror. Look into your eyes. Do you like what you see? Unfortunately, most of us don't. Some of us can't even look at ourselves. Why and how can this be changed?

Look into the mirror and say, "I love you! You're the only person who will truly love you. I'm freeing everyone of their responsibility to make you happy. I am grateful to share my life with you. I'm the one who takes care of you. I love brushing your teeth, combing your hair and washing your body. I love you so much that I even wipe your ass. What a nice ass it is! When you're hungry, I feed you, and when thirsty, I quench you. I buy you food, and comfortable clothes. Every line, mole and mark on you is awesome, and is what makes you who you are. Thank you for protecting me and showing me your love. Some call it fat, but we call it insurance. You rock and you're perfect. No one can love you like I can, and I do... lots. I'm going to feed you better, and exercise. We are going to laugh more. I'm going to stop being so hard on you. To celebrate us, we are going to get a massage and a new haircut. I know you won't last forever, and I will have to give you back some day. But until then, we are going to live, love and laugh."

Remember, you have to love yourself first, before you can unconditionally love another, or allow them to love you in return. So, start falling in love with yourself.

## ALIGNING AND PROTECTING

Visualize a white energy bubble all around you, making sure it encompasses your whole body like an eggshell. Let this force-field expand beyond your body a few feet. Visualize warm golden energy flowing from your heart, down your body and deep into the earth. Sense your feet becoming very heavy. Envision a cool blue light coming in through the top of your head and into your heart, connecting you to the centre of the universe. Now that you're protected and plugged in, anything that isn't resonating to a high vibration will be zapped off you. Visualize your aura pulsating, removing all negative thoughts, emotions, virus, and bacteria. Whatever doesn't resonate to your Divine Source can't hang around. Be gentle and loving, you're not on a war path of destruction. Now say, "I AM grounded, I AM protected, I AM free, I AM Love."

## QUICK POWER UPS

These quick power up exercises will ground, protect and empower you. They can be done on the fly. We can't always be in silence and meditating. Life happens. You can do these separately or in sequence. It depends on where you are, and how you need them.

## MORNING QUICKIE

When you first wake, and before getting out of bed, take a moment to do a quick body scan. Notice if there is any pain, stiffness or tension in your body. If you find any, breathe into it and do a quick body bath. Or, just send it immense love. You can do a quickie anytime of the day.

## LOCK N' LOAD

Take a deep breath in and hold... feel your feet... relax as you exhale. Become as heavy as you can, and allow the weight to build in your feet (this is grounding). As you inhale: raise your chin, pull shoulders your back, push your chest out, straighten your spine and pull your stomach inward. You're not a robot, so be graceful about it. Breathe deeply a few more times, slowly... feel yourself grounded.

## STOPPING TIME

Since time is perceived in the physical dimension, the only way to unhook from it, is to stop perceiving it with the mind. I found the best way to do this is to become aware of the body, and the space that it occupies—be in the present moment, and feel it. Once the mind gets involved, we lose the moment. So, make like a tree and *leave it*. If you look at a plant, you'll notice how it's just being. There is no mind, no thought, and no resistance—it is just being. I know when I'm allowing because I feel a buzzing energy all around me, and time seems to stop. I become aware of the space that allows objects to exist. I hear the silence behind the sounds that vibrate. Become the observer, witness and allow what is, without judgement, narrative, or resistance.

## REALITY CHECK

Repeat this as often as you can remember throughout your day: "I AM not this experience, I AM a witness, I AM the observer. All is perfect. I AM exactly where I need to be. I AM trusting the process. I AM grateful, I AM abundant, I AM joy, I AM love. I AM doing my best."

## MINDFUL

This means being mindful, not full of mind. Whatever you do, be aware of your actions. Doing so, automatically puts you in the present moment. When you eat, chew slowly, taste the food, and feel the textures and flavours swirling about in your mouth. Notice the movement of your jaw, feel how it slides down your throat and into your stomach. When you breathe, feel the air filling your lungs. Feel your diaphragm expand and contract as it draws in and expels the air. Be aware of your body as much as you can, no matter what activity you're engaged in. Use your senses to distill full awareness. There is a difference between using your senses, and them using you. When we can control them, they are wonderful to have. When they control us, we become their slave.

CHAPTER TWELVE

# THE ASCENT

*There is no never, can't you see? Our love is forever, and we're free. Excerpt from the song 'Forever' 1992 by Frank Di Genova.*

Each lifetime is a chapter in the story of our soul's journey. This may be the final chapter in The Ultimate Journey, however, it is not the end. This book is but a small facet of a diamond, one of many that glisten under the bright sun. It is a spark that beckons you to look within—to see the beauty that is waiting to shine—to blossom.

With every end there comes a beginning, and for each door closed another opens. You've heard these precepts before, yet have you pondered their deeper meaning? Do you have the courage to let go of the past? Do you have the trust to walk through the door and into the unknown? Do you have the strength to seek your truth, and to realize your true nature?

## METAMORPHOSE

Two years ago I was put to the challenge. Not once, but multiple times. I had to chose between hanging on to what was, or let it go. In one lunar year, literally everything that I had emotionally invested in, was taken from me. My mother died at sixty-eight, abducted by cancer. The family hair salon I'd taken on from my father, closed. It had been at the same location for forty-one years. All that remains now is a large hole in the ground. It is slowly being filled, so it can support a fifty-eight storey condominium. At eighteen, my son decided to move away from home and live in the city. He wanted to taste Toronto, living the bachelor lifestyle, and he'd be closer to his school. Unlike his father who commuted long hours, this wasn't an option for him.

In the dead of winter that year, I was invited up north to visit my soul tribe. On the long drive, I pondered on all that had occurred over the past two years, and throughout my lifetime. *Why was my life unravelling from every direction? What was happening to me?* I was losing my sense of self. *Where was the old me? Who was emerging?* Social events and *hanging with friends* no longer resonated. I just wanted to stay home. Everything was falling away. Nonetheless, I was looking forward to my well-deserved holiday the following week. I was going alone. It would be my second solo vacation. This time, it was with a suitcase and not a backpack! Trekking around Italy for three weeks had been fun, but not what I needed. This time I'd relax for six days on a beach in Cuba. *Why have I been single for so long? How many more weddings and parties did I have to attend, stag?*

I had been on the road for nearly an hour. It was dark, and the sun had set some time ago. The weather was bad, and visibility was low. It was cold and the snow was falling heavily. *At this rate, I wouldn't get there for another forty minutes.* My friends were waiting for me, dinner would be served upon my arrival.

I never liked being late—my track record was proof of this. The weather, and the fact that I worked that day, made me tardy.

I noticed the car's dashboard flickering, it would dim then illuminate. The windshield started to fog up, even though the defrost dial was set to maximum heat. Soon after, my headlights decided to create a romantic ambience in front of my car. *No, what's happening?* Everything was shutting down: heat wasn't blowing out through the vents, and the radio was fading. The car's electrical system was failing. I had to wind the window down so I could see, as the windshield was covered with a layer of condensation. I was lucky that I had manual windows! It was lights out. I turned off the radio, shut the vent and dashboard display. I had to preserve energy. I knew that if I stalled the car (manual shift) it wouldn't start again. I still had a way to go before I'd arrive at my destination. I had no gloves or a hat, and was freezing from head to toe. The road was slippery, and my body tense. My hands gripped the steering wheel way too tight. In addition, the power steering had gone weeks before, so it was difficult manoeuvring. *Thank God I'd changed over the old tires to new ones.* I had been driving on slicks a month before, they were smooth, to the bone. My car had travelled nearly four-hundred thousand kilometres and was over eleven years old. She was my trusted girl, and sadly wouldn't last forever.

I chanted every mantra I knew, imploring Source Energy to keep the car going. I gave her Reiki and even offered my own energy for her to use. Somehow, I made it to the exit, and off the highway. Most country roads don't have street lights, neither did this one. I felt the next level of panic kick in, realizing I was driving blind in the dark, and in a snow storm. By some means, which I'm certain were beyond the physical realm, I made it. I don't know how, but I did. Shaken and cold, I felt relieved and grateful to be greeted at the front door by my friends. With my adrenals shot and feeling drained, my body began to shiver. It would be the last time I drove that car. She passed away in the driveway. She'd given me her all, and had no more.

At the time, I didn't understand what was happening to me. Loss was occurring from all aspects of my life, and all at once. Even my cell phone stopped working. *Why? I hadn't dropped it. Why was I being targeted? Why was I being made to suffer and lose everything that I held dear?* I completely misinterpreted these events as a conspiracy plot against me. When in fact, it was a process of releasing the old and stagnant energy I had held onto. It had been my resistance to let go that had caused me the pain and suffering.

A year and a half later, I was again on my way to see some of my soul tribe friends. The weather was sunny and a balmy thirty degrees celsius. Unfortunately, this time it was me and not my car, that was under the weather. I'd woken that morning with a rawness in my throat, it was getting worse and pressure was also building in my sinuses. While enjoying the scenery on my long drive, I noticed the word *Mariposa* on a sign, to the side of the road. In Spanish it means butterfly. I didn't think much of it at the time. When I reached my destination, I bowed in gratitude, and thanked my new car for getting us both there safe and sound.

My cold had gotten worse, and my body was tired. *Was this really a cold, or was I integrating a shift?* I had all the symptoms, but it didn't feel like a classic cold.

I was resting in my sleeping quarters when I saw it—a mariposa. Made of metal wire, the insect empress hung directly on the wall at the end of my bed. The aha moment struck. *Was I in the chrysalis stage of transformation?*

When one goes through any type of change or transformation, it's not always an obvious or easy transition.

## WHO AM I?

*"Who am I without my money, job, status, or career? Who am I beyond all the human roles I play? Who am I without all the things I've acquired and held on to? Who am I when my body starts to age and wither away? Who am I underneath all the masks that I hide behind? What is my purpose, and why am I here? Will anyone remember me when I'm gone?"*

I've been asking these questions since before I can remember. Do you ask yourself the same ones? We came here with nothing, and will leave the same way. Even the container we've used for our physical body decomposes to nothing. This leads me to ask the question of why we still seek fulfilment and security through impermanent things?

We are not the body, nor the mind. We are the observer. Our intellect is what creates ideas and stories about who we think we are—the mind identifies and invests in these dramas. We are Source energy and therefore always connected to that Source. The ego is what gives us the illusion that we are separate. The waves in the ocean are expressions of our creative desires. There is no separation. We all have a kernel latent within us, waiting to awaken when we choose to arouse it. Maybe the time is now—after everything we've tried has failed. Who do we blame after all our excuses are gone, and everything has been stripped away? Many of us have a grave misconception that our Soul is lost or sick. This is not so. Our Soul doesn't need to be saved nor transformed. It is our ideas, thoughts and beliefs that need healing. Our Soul is waiting for us to smell its fragrance.

## UNCONDITIONAL LOVE

This journey isn't about attainting things, or knowledge. It's about realizing our true nature. We must be willing to unlearn everything we've been taught about what will give us fulfilment. We need to let go of all our attachments. The hardest passage is the one from the mind to the heart—it's the ultimate journey.

Our heart is a nuclear reactor of infinite power. It encompasses all the wisdom we are searching for. The mind is part of the illusion, it's a trap, unstable, and easily confused. It forgets, misinterprets, makes mistakes, and gets entangled by its own web of deception. The mind can only understand something conceptually, but until it's known in the heart, it's not truly known. The heart always knows, and cannot be outsmarted by even the sharpest mind. Constant and steady, it is love and wisdom. The mind can only comprehend facts and knowledge—intellectually.

Love is the most powerful force in the universe. Actually, it is the only force in the universe. It needs nothing, and is independent, non-dual and eternal. Unconditional love knows not of expectation, manipulation, or force. It dissolves shame, guilt, anger, and the root of all of them... fear. Love is acceptance, compassion of self and others. We are either in love or in fear, and it abides in the heart, not the mind. Many on the spiritual path are caught in the mind. They have an answer for every question, yet aren't any closer to awakening than those not seeking.

Can you love yourself? Can you look in the mirror and accept everything you see? We are what we are looking for. Everything is an illusion. It's imperative we stop looking for fulfilment with things or from others. When we realize what we are, the delusion falls away. We see ourselves in everything, and in everyone.

## THE RIGHT PATH

How will you know that you're on the right path? When it feels right. Things will feel good and flow effortlessly. If you encounter a lot of setbacks and conflicts, there is resistance on some level. Assess if it's the best course of action to take. The timing could be off, or it might not be in your best interests. All things come in Divine time. The *no pain no gain*, and *fight through it* statements are from the old paradigm. The new template is about flow, love and ease.

This doesn't mean to give up at the first sign of difficulty, or to fall into apathy. It's about going with the flow, like the river. When things keep messing up it's a flag indicating that you're not in alignment. Resistance creates blocks, and destroys our health and vitality. When something doesn't feel right, stop trying to fix it. Instead of complaining that it's not working, trust and surrender. When your fear has gone and you're no longer being triggered, you're on the right path. You feel it. You no longer take criticism personally and instead have understanding and compassion.

You're always on the right path and exactly where you need to be—even if you've screwed up a million times. It doesn't matter if your past is a disaster, it has brought you to where you are now. It has given you contrast, clarity, and a grand pallet of choices to choose new courses of action. Be grateful for all your experiences, and have no regrets. You did the best you could at the time. If you knew better, you would have done so. Let go of expectations, and stop being so hard on yourself. Who cares if you're not where you think you should be. You may not like it, but, there is reason why you're not.

## ONE OF A KIND

There will never be another like you again, ever. The universe never replicates itself. Each and every one of you is like a snowflake—no two are the same. So it's impossible to compare yourself to anyone. Why would you want to anyway? We're all unique and wonderfully different. We all bring something specialized to the world, to the collective. Homogenizing is for milk, not for replicating items on an assembly line.

We are limitless souls that are able to create, express and experience the life we choose. We're not here just to exist, pay the bills, and wish that we could be something greater. We're here to have fun and to explore this reality. Give yourself permission to do so. You don't need another's consent. Everyone has their own journey, let them enjoy it freely. Who are we to judge another's choices?

## THE PROCESS

Slowly, as we wake, we notice that we don't do certain things anymore. We lose interest in the things we once cherished—they become an afterthought. I never missed a Toronto Maple Leafs hockey game on tv. There would be times when I had to go to a wedding on a Saturday night and I'd bring a radio or small tv set so I could catch the game. It was Hockey Night in Canada, I could never miss that—even when it wasn't the playoffs! Now, I don't even subscribe to cable. Even if the game is on (free-to-air) and I tune in, I turn it off after a few minutes.

I'd like to caution that when we do embark on a path of self-discovery, our enthusiasm may at times be excessive. We may become gung-ho and lead the parade and start to preach. I've been there. This is another form of resistance—a refusal to accept what's not supporting our expanding consciousness. When I first became a vegetarian, I was giving sermons everywhere on why we should all stop eating meat. I wanted to make a difference. The only difference I made was pissing people off. Eventually, I stopped engaging and quietly went about my business. What I learned was, we lead by example.

*I have learned never to offer unsolicited help unless it is asked of you—no one likes being preached to. You picked up this book because you chose to. Conversely, you'd put it down if you didn't resonate with the content. If you're still with me, thank you.*

I've also realized that every problem is only my mind conjuring up a story around it. I still get caught, however, it's less often. When I do, I'm not so hard on myself. Fear is the architect behind everything that keeps me separated from my highest self. True confidence is not built on pride or based on ones corrupt sense of high self-regard. It is all mind-stuff and illusionary.

I get it, it's not easy when we experience losing something that we have identified with as being who we are. It can be an overwhelming and lonely path. The truth is that we're never alone, ever. One of the hardest things for me to do was to let go of everything. Not only what had happened in the last two years, but all the intangibles. The need for approval, the partying, the flirting, and the need to be the star of the show. They were my masks and my shield. Now however, being vulnerable has turned into my strength. Sometimes I question if it's all worth it. The answer is yes, it is worth it.

That doesn't mean that I still don't slip into old patterns. When I do, it isn't for long, and I am quickly reminded of why I've moved away from them. There comes a time when one stops putting their hand in the fire and then asks why their hand hurts. I can't fake it anymore.

I'm far from perfect, nor I am pretending to be. What has changed for me is that I am starting to love myself more unconditionally. I can see in others the same struggles that I've endured and continue to face. The difference is, I have learned compassion. This doesn't mean trying to fix anyone, it is about witnessing the process of what they are going through, and allowing. Compassion means being there when you are needed.

Writing this book has exposed me, I have nowhere to hide. The need to be accepted and fit in isn't as important to me now—being authentic is. There are no magic formulas or quick schemes on this journey. It is not a race, but a sojourn of the human race. We are not waiting for a miracle to save us. The miracle is inside, waiting to unfold. Slow down, listen to your breath, and feel the love in your heart.

## AWAKE

Awakening is initiated when we stop blaming, resisting, and being afraid. It begins when we start loving, allowing, and being grateful for all that is. Living spiritually doesn't mean being passive and positive all the time—it's about being authentic, transparent and vibrant. Awakening is the realization of being okay with whatever arises.

With each breath we take, we come closer to knowing our true nature. With each exhale, we release the layers of ignorance that stops us from knowing. No longer do we hide behind walls built from fear, a sense of incompleteness or mistrust. We watch as compassionate witnesses, without the need to control or fix what is happening. We respect the choices of how others want to walk their path—we are in service to them. As our light shines brighter, we become a lighthouse for the ships lost at sea—a beacon of light. The need to react subsides, and the desire to observe with love and compassion rouse.

## THE BUTTERFLY

There are four stages in which a butterfly has to go through in order to transform from an egg to an adult. It hatches from its protective shell and is birthed as a caterpillar. The multi-legged larva eats everything it can, to grow, feeding off the leaf that it was born on—leaving nothing in its wake. As it increases in size, it needs to molt because its exoskeleton doesn't expand—it outgrows itself. As soon as the caterpillar has fully grown, it forms itself into a chrysalis. Initially, it appears as if it's just resting, as no change is visible. Yet, on the inside, magic is happening—rapid transmutation. When it's time, it breaks free. The butterfly emerges with its newly formed wings folded against its body—they spread. The wings slowly fill with blood until the butterfly is ready to take flight—metamorphosis is complete.

What stage are you at? Are you ready to break free from your old and limiting form? Are you ready to be seen? Are you in position to spread your wings and show their brilliant colours. Are you ready to take flight?

## ÀSCENT

The bags of sand drop away, and our balloon rises higher in to the sky. We behold the vast landscape from a grander view. We are lighter, softer, yet stronger than we've ever been. The less force we use, the more powerful we are. The more we allow, the less we resist, and the clearer we see everyone as an expression of the Divine Source.

We begin to see ourselves as pieces of a grand puzzle—all fitting perfectly together. Each one is of equal importance. The concept of competition and the need to be better dissolves, and is no longer a popularity contest. Feeling love and compassion, we desire to serve others in their quest for awakening.

We are each an explorer, forging our unique experiences. Together, we can help each other co-create mutual experiences. We are always exactly where we need to be, and know this only when we trust the process. And when we live in awe and sense the wonder—like a child, we are then open to miracles.

Peace is always present. Worldly desire is what disrupts its flow. When there's no wanting, there is peace. Enjoy the moment, stop thinking, and allow it to unfold. What we truly desire is to reconnect with the knowing, that we are Divine Love, Joy, and Peace.

Thank you for reading.
Namaste
Frank

# SURRENDER

*1998*

*by*

*Frank Di Genova*

*Time slips away and gone is another day.*
*Where is this peace of mind I crave, that never seems to stay?*
*No matter what I do, and no matter what I say, it never seems to last,*
*it just slips into the past... away.*

*It's so hard to see, when emotions are blinding me, from the truth*
*that's inside of me, oh help me God to see. I don't want any sympathy,*
*I just want to be set free...*

*I surrender everything, all my joy and all my pain inside.*
*I surrender everything, take it all until there's no place left to hide.*

*I thought I knew the way, but my pride got in the way.*
*Now I must learn to let it go, and let it all flow.*
*I'm starting now to see, it was always inside of me, if I still my mind*
*I'll know, everything I need to Be.*

*I surrender everything, all my joy and all my pain inside.*
*I surrender everything, take it all until there is no place left to hide.*

# Thank you for reading this book

It is my deepest desire that this book has helped you in some way. If it has, and you want to help a loved one, a friend, or anyone that may be searching for inner peace, I'd love for you to help me in return.

I invite you to leave a review where you have purchased this book. If you know of anyone that would enjoy The Ultimate Journey, please share it with them.

I am deeply grateful.

Please visit my website at www.frankdigenova.com. You can read my blog, and sign up for my newsletter to receive information on upcoming events.

# Thank you